Praise for
Addiction in the Family—Now What?

"An emotional and educational ride—and a must-read for those individuals and families struggling with addiction, in order to better understand the process and gain wisdom to survive."

—Dr. Jon N. Rosenthal, DO
ENT Associates of South Florida

"If you are looking to understand the impact of addiction on the family, this book is a must. Lawrence Fish, RPh, shares from both his personal experience as a father of a daughter who struggles with addiction as well as from his professional perspective as a pharmacist and how imperative becoming educated on addiction is to be an effective player in the recovery process.

"As a licensed marriage and family therapist and mother of a son who has struggled with a heroin addiction for over sixteen years, I related to both 'Z' and her father's pain and suffering and the feelings of helplessness for both. I highly recommend this resource to any family member or professional that is looking to better understand that the process of recovery is not a linear one and often tumultuous and complicated. Fish accurately depicts the reality of the addiction from a family dynamic perspective. This guide is written with both passion and purpose to help anyone who loves and or is trying to help someone afflicted by the disease of addiction."

—Vincenzina DiSalvo, LMFT
Marriage and Family Therapist
Fort Lauderdale, FL

Addiction
In the Family

Now What?

Lawrence Fish, RPh

Copyright © 2022 by Lawrence Fish, RPh. All rights reserved. Published in the United States by Citrine Publishing, State College, Pennsylvania. Thank you for complying with international copyright laws by not scanning, reproducing, or distributing any part of this book in any form without permission, except in the case of brief quotations included in articles and reviews. For information, address Permissions@CitrinePublishing.com.

This book is intended to supplement, not replace, the advice of a trained health professional. If you know or suspect that you have a health problem, you should consult a health professional. The author and publisher specifically disclaim any liability, loss, or risk, personal or otherwise, that is incurred as a consequence, directly or indirectly, of the use and application of any of the contents of this book. This is a work of nonfiction. Nonetheless, some names, identifying details, and personal characteristics of the individuals involved have been changed. In addition certain people who appear in these pages are composites of a number of individuals and their experiences. The views expressed in this work are solely those of the author and do not reflect the views of the the publisher. The publisher is not responsible for websites (or their content) that are not owned by the publisher.

Library of Congress Cataloging-in-Publication Data

Fish, Lawrence
Addiction in the Family—Now What?

p. cm.
Paperback ISBN: 978-1-947708-75-4 · Ebook ISBN: 978-1-947708-79-2
Library of Congress Control Number: 2022918350
First Edition, October 2022

CITRINE PUBLISHING
State College, Pennsylvania, USA
(828) 585-7030 · www.CitrinePublishing.com

For Suzi

Contents

Foreword VII

Introducing The Fish Curve IX

First There's Shock, Then Nausea, Then Tears 1

Who Can We Trust? 11

The Hit 19

Stay Cool But Get Help 26

The Rehab Process 32

Home Again 51

Relapse 59

Rocky Times 81

The New Boarders 90

I Have My Home Back 101

The House Is Ours Again 113

The Concept of "Normal" 117

Sliding Along The Slippery Slope 123

Contents

Still More to Learn About the Disease 133

The First Phase of Treatment: Detox 138

The Treatment Center 143

The Halfway House 147

IOP: Intensive OutPatient 150

The Prognosis 153

A Deceptive Disease 155

Family Interaction 161

The Marchman Act: A Step in the Right Direction—Maybe 172

Relapse, Compassion Fatigue, and Putting
the Whole Picture Together 182

Am I Helping or Enabling? 187

The Journey Toward Long-Term Sobriety 191

Is the Epidemic Really New? 201

Epilogue: Effective Boundaries and Good News 213

Postscript 215

About the Author 217

Foreword

As a person in long-term recovery with 10,798,140 seconds *(for a human patient/client afflicted with the disease of addiction, fighting urges/cravings, and living with life on life's terms is often one second at a time),* and counting, of continuous and sustained recovery, I can relate to "Z," Lawrence Fish's daughter whom you will meet in this book. As a father of two beautiful, and emotionally messy daughters, I can relate to Fish. And as an Internationally Certified Addiction Professional and Mental Health Counselor, with over seventeen years of experience treating individuals who struggle with addiction/mental health disorders (I believe addiction should be categorized as a mental health disorder), and their families, I hope you can agree that I am a qualified expert in this arena.

I've read many books written about addiction. I've read journals and memoirs written by addicts that graphically describe the heinous, insidious nature of this disease and the mental prison that they are enslaved in. I've read heart-wrenching books written by parents who cannot save or protect their child from this monster! And I've read books written by my peers who fear that they are fighting a losing battle. However, I've never read a book that gives all three views, struggles and perspectives. I found myself crying over Z, laughing out loud at Fish's way of expressing his observations, and shaking my head over the unethical and ignorant role the medical profession and government has played in the evolution of this epidemic!

This book is a must-read for everyone because we all love someone like Z. This book is a guide for medical professionals, codependent/enabling family members and friends, and human patients/clients afflicted with the disease of MORE.

I whole-heartedly endorse this book and will be the first one in line to purchase a box for the families that I treat, and another box for the human patients/clients that I treat.

David Levin, LCSW, CAP, ICADC, QS
CEO/Chief Clinical Director, Legacy Healing Center
Margate, Florida
August 2021

Introducing
The Fish Curve

The Fish Curve evolved from my years of practical learning and speaking with families at addiction and recovery group meetings. It is presented here as a helpful device for you to orient yourself as to where you may be in the process of supporting a loved one through the addiction treatment and recovery process.

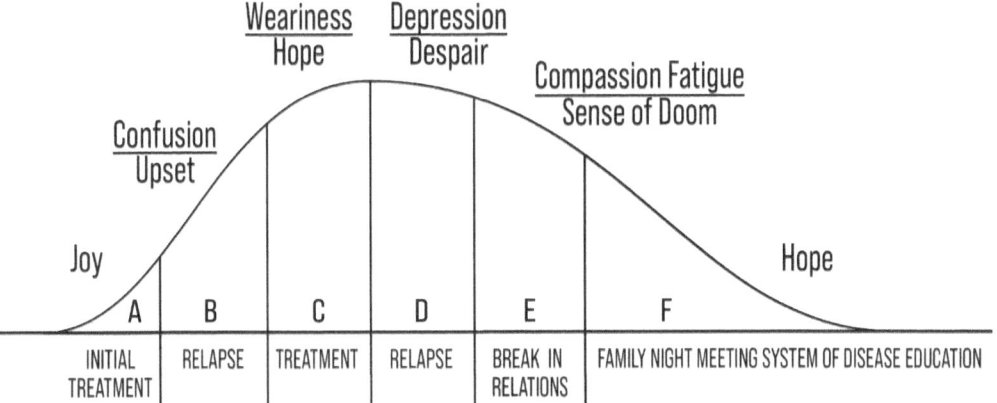

A) At this stage, you realize that your loved one is no longer getting high recreationally. They may agree to enter into treatment with a potential for success. You are elated. If there is a situation where you have an (almost) total lack of understanding of the disease, you are prepared for your loved one to leave treatment cured. Upon their release, you are in a state of joy.

B) After a period of time, you begin to notice signs of relapse potential. This is not always the case, as there are those that succeed on their first try. Your actions vary. Some accept this as the disease and attempt to get their loved one to re-enter treatment. Some may take this personally: "If they loved me, this would not happen." If love could prevent a relapse, chances are the success rate would be much higher. This could lead to disappointment, but at the first relapse it is still usually controllable.

C) If there is a return to treatment due to coercion on the part of family or a loved one, there is always hope and a chance for success. If the decision is on the part on the one suffering from the disease, there is a better chance for success.

D) Relapse is always a possibility. It should be remembered that this does not occur due to something you said or might have done. Although relapse should not be considered a part of recovery, it may be considered a part of the disease.

E) You realize that you either must accept your situation as the disease is in control over your loved one's thought process, or the other choice is to not accept this. The latter is a more feasible situation if you are together by marriage or siblinghood versus finding yourself in the role of a parent or guardian, serving a different function in your loved one's life.

F) Educating yourself is an important part of dealing with the disease. It could be the difference between keeping a marriage or family together. At this point, there is the potential for intermittent periods of joy and the realization that you no longer confuse the pain associated with the disease with a loss of love. At this point you realize that you must accept your situation, as it is out of you control. It is now a waiting game and a hoping one as you wait for your loved one to decide to enter into sobriety.

I hope this diagram is helpful to you. If you have any questions about it or the contents of this book, please feel free to email me at pharfish@aol.com. This is a challenging journey that I know in the depths of my soul. It is my hope that the pages ahead provide you support throughout the dark hours before the dawn.

—Lawrence Fish, RPh
Parkland, FL and Altoona, PA

First There's Shock, Then Nausea, Then Tears

It hits you like a ton of bricks.
You may think that your child is just an average teenager or college student or any student who studies and parties as millions of other children their age do. Or your family member, be it a husband, wife, sister or brother, may seem normal to you; perhaps due to a stressful home life or job pressures, they have a cocktail or smoke a joint "to relax" in the evenings. Suddenly, your world tumbles as you find out your child or family member has a *drug problem*.

How you find out can happen in different ways, none of which make you feel any better, although the scenarios might spark varying degrees of emotional intensity. The constants are the fear, shame, and perhaps guilt, but always the utter confusion as to what could have caused this. *What did I do to cause it and what should I do next?* One day your loved one, who you suspected was using drugs recreationally, as were a lot of people that you knew, appears to be managing their way through life and the next day you find yourself in a situation that leaves you barely able to cope with the reality of their addiction. Once the initial shock of this news passes, the situation might look something like this:

Scenario 1: The person you love sits you down and tells you they have a drug problem and they want to get help. This usually occurs *after* you have noticed that they have been getting high for a while but you figured that it was just a passing phase. Yours is one of the lucky families in this scenario. You are firm in your conviction that they do need help—denial is a major problem in this disease. It is imperative that you react rapidly as it is common for the addict to change their mind about getting help—sometimes faster than you can call the treatment center. This scenario is rare and precious: your loved one grew weary of the double life they were living and the lies they were telling.

Scenario 2: You get a call from your child or family member. They have been arrested. *Can you come to the courthouse and bail me out?* They are in trouble, but you are blessed because they are still alive and can get help. Denial remains a strong possibility for both of you. The upside to this scenario is that the court system has become more progressive and many jurisdictions have set up drug-court systems to deal with the problem in a knowledgeable manner. Your family member is usually given the options of going into treatment or doing jail time. Hopefully, treatment is the option that they choose. Your loved one is likely totally upset that they were incarcerated but they were "just having fun" and "there's nothing wrong," with them, it was "just an overly aggressive cop who should have just minded their own business."

You tend to agree with your loved one, though you are upset. Perhaps by agreeing, you are missing an opportunity to help them choose help. But, if you missed this opportunity, you are not the first to do so and you won't be the last. If you are on the right track, there is always the judge who, often through no fault of their own, dismisses the case on the grounds that this is their "first experience with the judicial system" and there is neither money nor room for their incarceration. And, by the way, they might be given a third option: their attorney may arrange for them to receive probation with the possibility that their record be expunged should this be their only arrest and they follow the rules humbly and properly. It is a mixed blessing but one worth accepting, assuming you and your loved one understand it as such. Sadly, in this scenario, we might again see that denial is an integral part of the systemic roots of this disease.

Scenario 3: You get a call from the police. Your child or family member has overdosed, is in the hospital, and you'd better get over to the emergency room as soon as possible. This is the most frightening—*are they still alive?* If they are alive, your sudden exposure to this disease can be likened to being dropped into a tub of ice water. The important thing to focus on is: if they are still alive, they can get help. The sad fact is that even though you have almost just lost your loved one, you and many family members may still believe it was "purely accidental" and again, we see denial running rampant in the family system.

Scenario 4: You open the door to your child or family member's room and find them laid out on the floor or bed as they have overdosed. You scream in panic and hopefully have the presence of mind to call for help. If they are still alive, they can get help and so can you—who, in the immediate moment, need it more than they do. In certain cases, a shot of Narcan can have them up and about quickly as if nothing happened, assuming (and these are huge assumptions) that there are no residual effects, that you *have* Narcan, and/or that the paramedics arrive in time. Oh, and yes, once you calm down, the chance for denial is still present: "this was not really the action of an *addict*. It was just a *bad choice* they made." By the time this rationalization process kicks in, you have seen your loved one dead (or as close to dead as possible with the possibility of resuscitation).

Hopefully 911 was called so that help is now on the way. Next, someone should start chest compressions. These will, if done properly, keep the blood flowing and help avoid brain damage. (By the way, if your loved one lives at home, you should invest in a doctor visit and obtain a prescription for Narcan nasal spray. If administered in time, it can save your opiate-overdosed loved one's life. Leave the box in plain sight so that the paramedics can see that you have administered a dose before they arrived.)

Scenario 5: Your child has overdosed and is dead. At this point the fight is over. You will most likely feel as if some or all of the responsibility rests upon you. Another denial option could be that it wasn't your loved one's fault, but rather *the crowd* that they had hung around with. There is not much I can say to make you feel differently as this is when a professional therapist is needed. All I can say is that *the addict is responsible for their addiction and actions, not the family members or anyone else.* This is something that no one but you and a therapist can deal with. Nobody can make the addict use or stop using. This is something that is at the sole discretion of the addict. If I had a magic wand, I would wave it and try to help each person affected by addiction to feel better, especially should Scenario 5 occur, but sadly, I don't have one. Grief counseling should be looked into at this time.

These are the hard realities of this disease. Until there is a crisis, most family members are aware that there are problems but deny the disease. Perhaps they compare their loved one's addiction to their own use of alcohol or marijuana. Until we learn to accept the fact that the family member suffers from a disease known as addiction, there is no way that we can be a part of the healing process. Your support increases their chances of success. One can be addicted to *any and all* drugs: be it heroin, alcohol, or caffeine. An alcoholic is indeed a drug addict as well.

Almost all drugs can be deadly if misused, and those that seem the least horrific are often the hardest to detox from.

If an addict attends Alcoholics Anonymous (AA) meetings, their discipline should be respected—it is the fellowship that they have chosen. Why is there reluctance to admit that a family member might be suffering from this terminal disease? Could it be shame? Could it be guilt? Could it just be the fact that we grew up in a generation that accepted getting high as a part of life? Why do we so often accept the blame for our family member's addiction, especially when they are our child? Perhaps it is our permissiveness or the fact that today, often both parents find it necessary to work. Nobody can tell what the reason for this pattern of thinking is. The important thing is to try to begin to understand that *the only person responsible for the addict's disease is the addict.* This disease affects not just the addict, but the whole family. Yes, family members can have a negative effect on the recovery process. But, remaining in the state of recovery is a discipline that your loved one must master on their own.

Growing up in the sixties might have made me a more relaxed parent. After all, we went to college where almost everyone smoked pot. It was the norm. We would head out to protests, and then we would come home, refresh ourselves, turn on the stereo, and have a party. Even those who didn't go to college also got wrapped up in the times and smoked daily. People you would never suspect indulged in this form of recreational activity. *Everyone* smoked pot. And now we know that our elected officials were among those who partook in this activity, too. There were many types of drugs available at the time, but for the most part, pot was the recreational-use-only drug. Smoking it was a form of rebellion with the added benefit of no hangover the next day.

Eventually, I began to notice a change in those around me and even in myself. We *had* to get high to party—not due to addiction, but because it was the thing to do. There was a cult-like aspect to it. Smoking pot became a part of the hippie anti-war counterculture. Most of us shared the long hair, the way we dressed, the head shops, the posters, the music, and the look of dismay we saw on our parents' faces when we spoke of the counterculture.

We had code names for it like Mary Jane, Boo, or doobie that made us sound like we were part of the counterculture and for sure, so cool. For the most part, for those that I knew, getting high was for recreational purposes and not a way to survive life. Our parents felt that it was a phase, a part of growing up that one had to go through while evolving into adulthood: a kind of rite of passage. For some, marijuana usage was kept secret so that their parents wouldn't think they were addicted to it.

At the end of the day, most of the pot smokers I knew grew up to become productive members of society. Perhaps many still smoke pot recreationally at a party or after work in place of a cocktail. There were those, however, who were high all the time, no matter what the occasion. Then there were those who made the move to opiates, barbiturates, and/or amphetamines, entering into the world of addiction. Some overdosed and died.

There are those who must smoke pot on a daily basis to "cope with life." It is my opinion—and I do not profess to be an addiction professional—that when you need a substance to cope with life then you have a problem.

I remember being asked once if I felt that oxycodone should be made a Schedule I drug. This would have put it in the same category as heroin and thus unavailable for prescription purposes. My reply was that it should be kept legal. When asked why, considering all it had caused, with so many people becoming addicts—including my daughter—my response was, "Why should those who require this narcotic analgesic for legitimate purposes be deprived of its availability because there are those who abuse it?" I feel that those in need should not be made to suffer for the abuser.

Perhaps it is true that most addicts started out using marijuana. It could also be that they started drinking wine or beer or vodka or any other legal substance capable of producing a hypnotic state. So why then do some end up hopelessly addicted to substances that others can use easily and safely? This, some years ago, was an unanswerable question to which only theories existed. The "upside" to this insidious epidemic is the increase in research brought about by the increase in the number of addicted family members. Yes, I say family members because I feel that addicts, while on a run, have no negative emotions other than perhaps that imposed by family. If they were able to continue to use without impunity, or not feel the guilt and shame that eventually becomes self-imposed by their knowing that their loved ones are suffering while they are using, they would be happier than a fly in a sewer treatment plant.

In 1990, addiction was finally recognized as a disease in the Americans with Disabilities Act. The government reacted by building treatment centers, creating drug courts, and providing grants for research—although not often voluntarily. Although North America is in the middle of an addiction epidemic, the majority of taxpayers are not directly affected by it and thus often object to tax increases to pay for treatment facilities. The electorate are caught between those who want and those who don't and therefore finances for treatment are at a minimum.

Opiate addiction has existed for years but since it was mostly confined to the inner-city ghettos nobody cared much about it. Due to mistreatment of black drug abusers by police in the inner city, there is a reluctance to report overdoses and prescription abuse. To supplement or provide income, there are large inner-city sales forces for heroin and crack. These are largely due to the racial inequalities in the mainstream work force. According to Kristina Murray, this combination has led to a significant increase in both the consumption of, and death due to, overdose from drugs.[1] Now that the problem has reached more affluent suburbs, it has finally become called an epidemic.

Research leans towards this disease being a genetic type of disorder.[2] The government has set up programs to treat addicts but these are usually underfunded as the constituency feels that they are not dealing with someone with a disease, but rather someone who is having a "good time at our expense." It is not until this often-terminal disease hits close to home that opinions change, and since the recent oxycodone epidemic, (that has reached epic proportions) the public has finally spoken out and all levels of government have responded—but in a still less-than-appropriate manner.

The fact that the AMA declared alcoholism a disease in 1956 and officially deemed addiction a disease in 1987[3] doesn't resonate with everyone. Noted Canadian Neuroscientist Marc Lewis claims that although addiction leaves ruts in the brain, these can be overcome, much like marks left upon the brain by cravings for food and other desirable things can be. It has been my experience from attending Family Night meetings for more that thirteen years that parents and family of loved ones suffering from this disease often begin their journey with the resentment of feeling that their loved one is *choosing* to use. My feeling is that over time one should begin to see the helplessness of the addict who tries to seek sobriety without the help of professionals. Dr. Lewis

---

1   *The Tinge of the Drug Crisis: Black Americans and Opioids,* Kristina Murray, September 11, 2018
2   Bevilacqua, L., & Goldman, D. (2009). Genes and addictions. *Clinical pharmacology and therapeutics, 85*(4), 359–361. https://doi.org/10.1038/clpt.2009.6
3   Leshner A. I. (1997). Addiction is a brain disease, and it matters. *Science (New York, N.Y.), 278*(5335), 45–47. https://doi.org/10.1126/science.278.5335.45

compares the feelings that an addict has for drugs with those of someone who breaks up with a loved one.

Perhaps I am being too hard on the government. Perhaps the lack of reaction is due to a lack of knowledge or understanding of this disease. Perhaps it is due to a lack of desire to get involved in a situation that could bring about litigation on the part of those medical practitioners who could be charged with violating their professional codes. When it comes to professional issues such as the legitimacy of when and if narcotic pain relievers may or should be dispensed, it has been my experience as a licensed pharmacist that there is a hesitancy to have law enforcement intercede. At this point, law enforcement is limited to ascertaining whether the practitioner is following proper medical procedure as far as examining the patient to see if they are *actually in need of medication*. It was found that the pill mill doctors were not doing proper physicals and this is what eventually led to arrests. At present, there are still many physicians who prescribe legal opiates to those who suffer from the disease of addiction, but they are now smart enough to perform a proper examination, thus circumventing the law. However, I feel those in charge can take the hit for not learning about it, and not understanding how this affects addicts, their families, the economy, and our society as a whole.

As previously mentioned, the sixties was known for its rebellion. There were the anti-war protests, the psychedelic music and the turn-on, tune-in, drop-out newfound lifestyle. Along with this came the use of marijuana by so many of my generation. Since this drug was not legal, the use brought about an increased feeling of the counterculture. Pot was used with no fear of addiction as the word was it was harmless. We had no fear of addiction and many of our parents too accepted this theory. For most of us, the regular use of this intoxicant faded into a casual-use substance, such as a replacement for wine at a party. For many others, the regular use of this substance led to addiction without their even realizing they were addicted, until something brought about a consequence—perhaps getting caught smoking on the job, an arrest, or a wife or husband who could no longer put up with trying to converse with a spouse who was always too high to respond in a proper manner, resulting in a breakup of a relationship. Slowly, I began to notice people were no longer around. I grew up in the Rockaways, a beach resort in the summer but a small town during the off season where we all at the least knew each other. So, if you didn't see someone for a period of time, they were either away at school, moved or something was wrong. It was still a ways off before I would slowly begin to see marijuana use as a drug to be concerned about. For this reason, many families reacted very slowly, or not at all, upon hearing that their loved one was partying and using intoxicants on a consistent basis.

We are now faced with an addiction epidemic. I do not attribute this entirely to the use of marijuana, though I have come to realize over time that this drug is a gateway drug for many and is actually quite addictive, contrary to this controversy among many users. Still, many parents feel guilt for their lack of knowledge, believing that they could have prevented their loved one's addiction if only they had known. Could this be true? Well, let's take a better look at the situation. According to some, today's marijuana is different from that of the sixties, as horticulturists have developed more potent varieties of cannabis sativa. Regardless, the problem remains the same, because the substance is still being used for the same purpose as before, namely escapism and avoidance, which we cannot *avoid*.

One of the reasons that marijuana users believed this substance to be non-addicting was that they knew little about the dynamics of addiction. This is because the addictive dimension of this intoxicant hovers beneath the radar of those who are intoxicated primarily because they are in an altered state of intoxication. Meanwhile, if they are not intoxicated at the time, a sensitivity that would otherwise alert them to the presence of addiction, such as desire for more of the substance, would be obscured by their incapacity to think clearly or rationally, particularly if their drug dealer filled their mind with notions that they needn't be concerned because in their words, "Believe me man, dope (or weed) just isn't addictive!" And those who are not familiar with the obvious withdrawal symptoms associated with opiates, benzodiazepine amphetamines and alcohol, may not know any different and thus are not aware of the need for detoxification. The irony of the whole situation is that as you become more mentally impaired by the drug, you consequently become less capable of recognizing the impact the substance is having over your thoughts and feelings and are thereby unaware of the contrast.

But the key to treatment is not just the detoxification process. Shame on me—this is a very important part of treatment. Yet the physical detoxification process is only the first part of treatment and not something that is easily forgotten. The patient is ill, feeling severe nausea, cramps, aches and pain. This passes in a week or two, although the actual detoxification process, research shows, can last for months. Once addicted, your loved one will experience cravings, urges, and drug dreams. This psychological part of recovery lasts forever. So yes, marijuana definitely falls into the addictive drug category. The fact that it is thought to be "not harmful" and "non-addictive" by so many makes the drug all the more dangerous. For those new to addiction, this lack of recognizable withdrawal symptoms tends to confirm what other users say about their usage of marijuana. The truth is, your loved one will definitely experience some psychological changes during, and after, the detox. There will be a desire to use the drug, and perhaps depression or a change of personality. There is usually a considerable reduction of these symptoms when properly treated by a knowledgeable treatment physician.

Do I think that the government is wrong for legalizing marijuana for medical reasons? No! There is a place for this drug in the treatment of certain medical indications. Do I think that the government is handling this in a satisfactory manor? No. Medical marijuana should be controlled by medical professionals. Marijuana for social use too should have its controls, just as alcohol does.

Who Can We Trust?

We are led to believe that the government is here to help protect us from the scourge of the drug pusher. We hear talk of the terrible drug cartels and how our borders are open cesspools, inviting the mules that smuggle these horrible drugs across them. We are told that gangs are turning our streets into open flea markets where our loved ones can wander about, shopping for heroin, crack cocaine, meth, or any other drug that one might think to purchase.

Watch one of the many police docudramas that deal with drugs and you'll see the perception the average citizen—who has not been touched by this disease—has of the problem. The undercover police officer drives an unmarked car up to the dealer standing on the street, purchases a rock, and suddenly the screen explodes with police. They swarm all over the dealer, throwing him to the ground, slamming his face and head against the concrete, cuffing him then taking him away. We are led to believe that something wonderful has been done to make our streets safe from the scourge of addiction.

One of the main causes of the opiate epidemic was actually pill mills. They have been around, in one form or another, since the 70s. They have been called different names but basically what they have done is provide a source of drugs, on a quasi-legal basis, for those who want to get high, whether socially or to feed their addiction. There are also methadone clinics where someone who suffers from the disease of addiction can pick up a day's supply of methadone—this is supposed to help them control their disease.

However, there is/was much abuse and although they still exist, they are not the preferred method of treatment.

Then there was the "stress clinic." You could walk into a clinic where there was a doctor who knew nothing about stress, had a copy of the book *Sybil*, a story about a woman who suffered from multiple personality disorder, on the shelf in a feeble attempt to confer a professional appearance to the clinic, and would purchase a prescription for a month's supply of quaaludes and a stress vitamin. There was usually no exam and cash was required. Eventually these clinics were shut down and many of the doctors and owners were arrested.

More recently, the headlines and news networks have covered pill mills. A patient could walk into a clinic, claiming back pain, migraines, or any other type of "unprovable" pain, and pay cash for a prescription that would put an elephant down. Typically, there would be 180 tablets of 30 mg of oxycodone, 120 tablets of 15 mg of oxycodone, 60 tablets of 10 mg methadone or 60 tablets of 350 mg of Soma (carisoprodol), a muscle relaxant that replaced quaaludes after they were taken off the market. These mills would see over a hundred patients a day. As the local pharmacies, including the chains, became too afraid to keep filling these prescriptions, clinics opened their own dispensaries. Eventually, the government began to close them down.

At the height of the pill mill crisis, before the scat hit the fan, I was politically active. Though we tried to highlight the problem, there was very little action taken against those doctors prescribing for the pill mills. It was not until parents began to realize that their children were full blown addicts that our elected officials responded and begin to close in on these licensed drug pushers. The concept that a licensed medical doctor with the power to *prescribe medication legally* was committing a crime against our families was far more devastating to imagine than the ghetto pusher that we saw on the television. I often ask myself, what happened to our television coverage? Back in the less-sophisticated days of early TV, investigative reporters would have covered these stories and exposed the doctors and the plague that they created.

Once the headlines were over I, as a pharmacist, found that

the government did too little, too late. Once this disease takes hold, there is no cure. Like type 1 diabetes, addiction is an incurable disease and like cancer, can be a terminal one. Unlike type 1 diabetes, this is a disease that you bring upon yourself, and unlike cancer, with some exceptions, it is one that with help you can control the outcome of. Perhaps, for this reason the addict is looked upon differently than other disease sufferers. We, the citizenry, have been raised with a feeling of hierarchy: having wealth puts you above the uneducated and poor. When we arrest the person in the ghetto with pants hanging halfway down their ass selling crack, we cheer the basis for a successful docudrama.

But a doctor sells prescriptions (combinations of opiates, benzodiazepines, and intoxicating muscle relaxants) to our children for $150.00, wears a shirt and tie, displays his diploma, and we are shocked and saddened when the DEA arrests them. They see perhaps a hundred people or more a day, most in their late teens to their early thirties, and in all cases the office refuses insurance—cash-only payments allowed. Once the crackdown began, we saw this nightly on the network news. They would show the cars parked in the strip malls with license plates from all over the country, the patients would visit several clinics daily before returning to their home state where they would use and/or resell the drugs for $20 a tablet or more.

Addiction advances, if left untreated, much like a cancer. Cells that don't belong in our bodies replicate uncontrollably when one has cancer. Addiction, on the other hand, alters thought processes uncontrollably in our brain, thus causing the addict to bring about destruction to their body. I've often heard family members state that they are thankful that their family member is addicted to pills and not heroin. Obtaining pills such as oxycodone is a starting place for most suburban opiate users. To refer back to my previous pill mill example, the person "looking to party" goes to a doctor's office with $150.00 cash and purchases an assortment of medication that, taken together, would put an elephant to sleep forever. The upside is that they usually share these at a party or gathering—initially. As their addiction gets worse, the amount of drugs needed to produce the desired effect increases. This happens to be one of the reasons addiction was classified as a disease. "Tolerance" is the technical term for this. Tolerance refers to the increase in the amount of drug necessary to produce the effect that the drug *used to have*.

Rather quickly, users need to sell some of the pills so that they can pay for the office visits since the doctor is too smart to accept insurance. Also quickly, they need to *use all of the pills*. Welcome to the world of addiction. As the addiction progresses and tolerance builds, so does the need for money. It runs out quickly, but often there is a friend who says "there is a guy I know who sells better stuff for $5 or $10 a bag." The addict tries them and likes them better than the pills from Dr. Feelgood. Now they are what the family recognizes as an addict, thanks to the good Dr. and many poor decisions on the addict's part—no one forced them to see the doctor.

We now see why there is a heroin epidemic across the nation. Whose fault is this? The addicts', of course, but you may also ask what role the government played in allowing this drug to become available so readily. I wonder if the name Hammed Karzai strikes a bell? Remember the gentleman that we put in charge of Afghanistan after the war? His brother is the largest Poppy grower in the world.[4] The United States allowed poppies to be grown in Afghanistan by the farmers so that they can survive economically. Do you think that your government was unaware of this fact before setting up the new government in Afghanistan? If I know about it, I'm sure they did, too.

Most doctors do not know how to treat this disease unless they have taken special courses in addiction detoxification and treatment. The usual method the doctor uses to treat addiction is to replace one drug with another. While this has its place in the detoxification process, it should be used with extreme caution as we now see Suboxone maintenance used as a method of treatment for addicts that are categorized as chronic relapsers. (I'll explain that in the coming pages.)

---

4   Risen, J. (2008, October 4). Reports Link Karzai's Brother to Afghanistan Heroin Trade. *The New York Times*. https://www.nytimes.com/2008/10/05/world/asia/05afghan.html.

So now you know that your loved one will have no problem acquiring their drug of choice. Let's consider the most well-known of addictive drugs: heroin. Add an "e" and the definition becomes a woman with the attitude of a hero. A hero or heroine is someone who will enter into the picture to save the day. Now, you may ask as many before you have, how could such a devastating drug have gotten such a positive name?

Well, after World War I, when so many wounded soldiers came home addicted to morphine, heroin was the "miracle drug" that—in the words of Alex Gringhaus, my medicinal chemistry professor at the Brooklyn College of Pharmacy—was "going to free them from their addiction." Clearly not learning from this mistake, the drug companies set out to find another way to save the world—this time from the devastation of heroin addiction. Low and behold, after years of research, the next savior to come along was methadone. One has only to speak with one who frequents a methadone clinic to see how successful that was. Not only is methadone a strong intoxicant, it is also frequently used to barter, in the pill or biscuit form, for heroin. The bartering of methadone was so prevalent that eventually the 40 mg biscuit was withdrawn from retail sale.

Just like back in post-war days, as heroin addiction was harder to treat than morphine addiction, so too is methadone addiction harder to treat than heroin addiction. Especially as far as detoxification and recidivism is concerned. Once again, we learned nothing from our past experience. Have we finally given up on replacing one drug for another as a form of treatment for addiction? Of course not; after all, why would we choose to lose an opportunity to treat addicts in this most lucrative manner? Yes, we now have another drug to try. Suboxone is another form of treatment (drug) that allows the addict to function so that they can work and maintain a somewhat normal existence. Oddly enough this, to a certain extent, does work. The drawback is that usually the addict is required to have a monthly visit to their doctor to get a new prescription. These visits are for the purpose of getting a new prescription, and a minimal examination is done to meet the legal obligation of the law. Perhaps seeing the doctor monthly initially is a good practice, but as time goes on this can become cost prohibitive and Suboxone is a controlled class of drug that allows for renewals. As the doctor gains confidence in their patient, they should write for renewals so that the visits become more affordable. The prescription is also very expensive and frequently not covered by insurance. It is also addicting, with an ability to create a euphoric sensation if abused and harder to get off of than heroin. Lastly, it is often sold to other addicts, the proceeds then used to buy heroin. These things aside, if taken properly, one can probably function properly when using Suboxone.

But, would you want to go through life addicted to an expensive drug with unknown side effects and a monthly visit to a doctor to acquire a prescription? Both methadone and Suboxone are supposed to be used as a taper form of medication. This means that the patient is started off on a certain dose and that dose is reduced slowly over time until the addict no longer suffers from cravings that they feel they can't control and they then become drug free. As of late the addiction doctors have been prescribing Suboxone and methadone as a maintenance drug—there is no tapering (slow reduction) of the dose. If taken correctly, under the supervision of a legitimate addiction doctor, the addicted person can function in a normal manner. The drawback is that your loved one is still a functioning addict who if or when they miss a dose will begin the process of withdrawal. There is also a potential for abuse as a potentially euphoric compound is being given to a person who suffers from the disease of addiction. If an addict happens to find a legitimate addiction doctor they will only prescribe refills for the patient once a sense of trust has been established.

The bottom line is that at this time the best method of dealing with this disease is for your loved one to enter into treatment to get off of all drugs. This however, is not an easy task. Hopefully this book will be helpful and provide support for you but when this disease affects a family, reactions vary drastically. Just keep in mind that you are not alone. You must try to react in a rational manner, and most important, there is help out there for both the addict and the family members. This disease affects the whole family with anger, devastation, guilt, and shame. At the very least, I hope to help eliminate the shame and guilt: the place for shame and guilt is upon the shoulders of the addict when they are using; hopefully it *not there when they have made the decision to get help*. After the decision has been made to get help, it is a time to be proud—for both the addict and the family. For the first time since the addiction process started, the addict has taken a positive step and they should hold their heads up and be proud. Unfortunately, being sober allows them to remember the negative actions that they have committed while using and therefore, this is usually a time of great shame which, if not addressed, can lead to relapse. This is a hard time for the addict so hopefully they can count on their family's support.

So, who can we trust? Groups such as Alcoholics Anonymous (AA) or Narcotics Anonymous (NA), and many other fellowships have grown out of the need to answer this very question. Your family member or loved one is now attending meetings to help in their recovery, but are you? I feel that it is very important for your recovery to attend meetings also; meetings such as Al-Anon or Nar-Anon are 12-step meetings for families that are similar to the meeting that your loved one attends. Like their meetings are helping them, they will help you in your recovery too.

Yes, I know when I speak about "your recovery too," it may invoke feelings of anger or fear. The fact is, you have strong emotional ties to your loved one or you wouldn't be reading this book. You have just gone through a period of stress while your loved one was on a "run" (a term used to designate when an addict is in active addiction) and now that they are in treatment you either fear what will come in the future or suffer from some sort of shame or guilt. Maybe you realize it and won't admit it. You do have a problem. My personal feeling is that when we have a loved one in active addiction we suffer more than they do. They get high and hide their emotions. We have to deal with ours. So don't be ashamed to admit to yourself that you do need help—and attend a meeting. They say it may take six meetings before you begin to realize the benefits. You might also want to attend an AA or NA meeting to see what addiction is about, when the addicted person is in recovery. You can just Google the name to find a meeting in your area that is open to anyone.

At first most family members are reluctant to attend meetings as they are afraid of the unknown and can suffer from terminal embarrassment. Surprisingly, this disease has become so commonplace that there is hardly a family that doesn't have some member affected by it. So don't be surprised if you do attend an Al-Anon, Nar-Anon, or whatever-Anon meeting and bump into someone that you know. As confidentiality is a key factor to be maintained at these meetings, not sharing any knowledge of who attends is key. You will meet a group of people who are there to help you. They will help you through some trying times and teach you how to live your life in a meaningful and functional way, which is not an easy task.

Friends and family members may offer assistance and advice but it is those who have lived through the crises that you are facing that can help you the most. Like NA and AA, Al- and Nor-Anon provide literature to read and steps to follow, as well as traditions and sponsors. If this seems complicated, keep in mind there are people there to help you along your path to recovery. Yes, as a family member you too must recover from this devastating disease as you are forced to see things and live with situations that you probably never thought would affect your thinking process. Now that you've been affected, you too have the opportunity to get help. Like the addict, the help is there but you must make the decision to accept it and take action to seek it out.

The Hit

As a child, my daughter had everything going for her. She was beautiful, exceptionally intelligent, and possessed a strong personality. There was never any doubt in my mind that success would be hers for the taking. In middle school she was inducted into the honor society, obtaining straight A's the entire year. As she was the youngest of our four daughters, we did have a tendency to overindulge her whims—perhaps that is true of how most parents treat their youngest child? Not all overindulged children, however, end up addicts—spoiled perhaps, but not addicts.

From early on, I suspected my daughter was getting high. Unfortunately, there was an irresponsible man down the block who allowed the neighborhood kids to get high at his house—perhaps because his child suffered from a terminal disease. I didn't like it, but at that time I owned my own pharmacy, worked long hours, and was politically active—all of which took up a lot of my time. Thus, I never really knew to what extent she was using. I figured it was a weekend thing. I had no idea that she was sneaking out of the house nightly to join her friends at this guy's house. Because I had smoked pot (and if that was all she did well, no big deal!) I cruised along that river in Egypt. You know the one: Denial.

Maybe I was vicariously reliving my youth. I did speak with her regularly about the dangers of addiction and how once the line is crossed, you can never cross back. I never had any inkling that smoking pot would lead her to bigger things. Naïvety is perhaps the greatest fault a parent can possess. After all, she was in high school and *all* the kids were smoking pot.

In tenth grade, she seemed to drift away from academics and move toward the partying crowd. I again felt that this was something that would be overcome as she matured and she would eventually find her way back to the path of academics, much as I had in college. Looking back, the signs of drug abuse were present. But sadly, a parent rarely knows what is going on until the first crisis arises. Also, most people believe that *addicts don't come from good families.* Alcoholism possibly, but drugs are associated with bad people in bad neighborhoods. Again, beware the wrath of naïvety and ignorance of this disease.

Life was going along fairly smoothly; my daughter had graduated from high school and was attending college. Her grades were only just "fair" but I attributed this to the fact that she still had not decided on what she wanted to do with her life. She would come home from class, do her work, and leave to meet her friends. Nothing seemed strange at all. After several semesters of floundering, she decided to become a chef after a little push—or perhaps a shove—from her dad. She excelled, graduating magna cum laude from the culinary institute she attended. I couldn't have been prouder. After working for awhile, she felt that being a chef was perhaps too strenuous and management might be more her style, so she decided to return to school, achieving a four-year degree and graduating cum laude. Things were going great.

Upon graduation she applied for several positions but eventually returned to the kitchen. The job market was bad, the country was in a recession, and it seemed that the only recreation the populace was partaking in was the occasional trip to a restaurant. Though she was fortunate enough to land a somewhat decent position in the kitchen, a green chef, that is, one who is just starting out, makes only slightly more than a dishwasher. If, however, you have the passion and work hard this can become a very rewarding—and exhausting—career.

At this point she was living at home so although the income was weak, so were her expenses. These consisted of student loans and a car payment. She consistently made both and I, once again, was very proud. She had met a guy in school and the relationship seemed to be going well.

At about this time, she started mentioning that she was also going to "visit with a friend's brother." I asked if she thought this was right, since she had a boyfriend. She claimed that one was a boyfriend and the other was just a friend from back in her high school days. It made sense to me so the subject was dropped. One day she brought this "friend" home and the only thing I knew for sure was that her boyfriend seemed much more respectable than her friend.

He appeared to have trouble both walking and talking. He tried to be polite and friendly but was promptly whisked into her room. After a short period of time they reappeared, said their goodbyes and left. When she got home that night I asked what the problem was with her friend. She acted confused. "What do you mean?"

"He seemed to be a bit stoned." She said that he suffered from a seizure disorder and that he took high doses of anticonvulsants to control it. Being a pharmacist, I knew seeming stoned could be a potential side effect of these drugs. I was also was suffering from tertiary denial, so I let the subject drop. I couldn't help but think that seizure disorder aside, he still didn't appear to be the kind of person I might choose for a son-in-law. For some reason I had a strong feeling that I should lock away our worthwhile possessions. After I was called a snob, I retreated to my television that I now used as my martini. Snob or no snob—this guy did not seem right. I tried to envision how I might have appeared to the parents of someone I had dated back in the sixties. This, however, was not the sixties.

Life with her supposed boyfriend pushed the limits; sometimes he slept over. When I was dating my wife, that kind of thing seemed fine to me, but watching it happen with my daughter was definitely bothersome. However, he was a refined man who treated her with respect and I appreciated that. He was also well educated and had a potential career. From what I saw, he was quite talented in his chosen field and could be a good husband, father, and provider someday. So, like any self-respecting parent who grew up during the time of free love during the sixties, I just chewed an antacid and accepted my fate as the father of four daughters. But slowly I began to notice certain signs that I had previously been great at ignoring and putting out of my mind.

Being a pharmacist, I would often see people trying to obtain opiates such as oxycodone, methadone, and hydromorphone (Dilaudid) with the aid of a doctor's prescription—legally, of course. Usually these opiate prescriptions were accompanied by prescriptions for benzodiazepines—Xanax (often referred to on the street as Xanibars or just Bars), Valium (diazepam), and Ativan (lorazepam). All that was needed was a doctor who was either duped by these ever-so-clever and cunning patients or was in the profession to make a lot of money and had no morals. The patients getting these meds usually had trouble speaking or walking or both. Their claims were bad teeth, herniated discs, migraines, or any cause of pain requiring an opiate to both relax their minds and muscles. Their words would slur as my daughter's sometimes did. I would sometimes find her asleep on the couch—it did not appear to be a normal sleep. When I mentioned this to my wife she would respond, "The girl has a rough job"—a valid statement.

When she first started, she did prep work that meant she had to be at work early so she could begin the process of getting food ready for the chefs who actually cooked the meals. Most new chefs start with prep work and climb the ladder from there if they're good. Fatigue is not an uncommon part of the job. So I figured that after a hard day at work, smoking a joint was not the most disastrous thing one could do.

Meanwhile, I began to notice the proliferation of the infamous pill mills. People would come into the pharmacy with prescriptions from pain centers for unusually high amounts of opiates—usually oxycodone, benzos (slang for specific anti-anxiety agents classified as benzodiazepines which have the potential to intoxicate on their own), and opiates for breakthrough pain such as Dilaudid or methadone. My initial reaction was a verbal "Holy shit, this could kill a horse."

The pharmacist does not have to take courses in criminology to see what is happening in their pharmacy. Initially someone enters their pharmacy acting as though they are in severe pain with several prescriptions from a physician. It is possible to mistake them for a legitimate patient. Soon, the word gets out that the pharmacy stocks the drugs prescribed and there is an ever-increasing parade of juvenile patients who are in "severe pain."

At first, seeing the patient enter the pharmacy using crutches or a walker, the typical pharmacist fills these prescriptions. They call the doctor's office to verify the authenticity of these prescriptions, obtain a diagnosis that seems to be legitimate, and then enter this information onto the prescription. Once that *one* prescription is filled, the word gets out onto the street that "someone got some oxy" and suddenly there is a procession of young, healthy patients limping into the pharmacy. It is best practice to call the DEA to verify if these are legal prescriptions. (Actually, before this step the pharmacist should already professionally realize that something is not right.) The pharmacist is usually told that if the doctor is licensed and has a DEA number that the prescription can be filled. So, they continue to fill these prescriptions and for the first time, begin to see a respectable profit (the pharmacy business is a very tough, low-profit one for the independent—contrary to popular belief). One must wonder at what price this profit comes. At professional pharmacy meetings, the pharmacists who own stores may be speaking among themselves about how the good old days have once again returned. No one is totally innocent. Both the independent pharmacy owners and the chain pharmacists, for whatever reason, fill these prescriptions, knowing that to some extent what they are doing is wrong.

Politically, I tried to fight the offices where doctors used their license to act as pushers. I would ask the elected officials, who would show up at meetings to speak to club members, if they would do something about this situation. The response would be a "yes" and then nothing was done or, "It is a matter for the DEA and police to handle."

The clinics were, however, following a protocol that kept them just on this side of legal and none of the politicians seemed to want to get involved. All I can tell you is that at that time, pill mills were going "unnoticed," and the number of children who were becoming addicted was not realized. It was only the pharmacists and the doctors who wrote the prescriptions who could see the increase in youngsters and adults coming in with these prescriptions…and perhaps the parents that knew what was happening. Those most responsible were the doctors who prescribed these medications, the manufacturers who made (and still make) huge profits, and those pharmacists who specialized in opening stores just for this purpose.

One day I came home from a meeting and my wife looked distressed. She told me to sit down, that she had gotten some bad news. I sat. She told me the police had just called and said that although there was nothing that they could do to her legally (as she had prescriptions for her drugs) our daughter was stoned and had a definite problem and they felt they should let us know. My wife thanked them and waited for me to return. We then waited for Z to return home.

When the realization first hits, my reaction was shock. Everything I'd ever learned or saw about addiction was that this was a *ghetto problem*. I worked hard, saved money and moved to a nice neighborhood with good schools and I thought that while the kids may still end up smoking some pot, hard drugs and/or addiction is something that I would *never have to worry about*.

What did I do wrong?

Yes, it is natural to blame yourself as I once did, especially not having any knowledge of the disease. *Perhaps I devoted too much time to work and politics? Perhaps I should have been home more so that I could have seen this coming and prevented it?* And so, I sat there with my wife, awaiting our daughter's return. I tried to think rationally, but nothing made sense. *What do I do?*

As I sat there waiting, I began to feel sick to my stomach. As a pharmacist I knew the seriousness of this disease. But I was soon to find out *how little* I knew about it. We knew we had to get help, but *what do you do? Who do you call?* I tried to figure out a proper reaction to this situation. *Do I rant and rave? Do I threaten to turn her into the police? What was the correct reaction?* I quickly realized that, even being a pharmacist, everything that I believed I knew about this problem was totally inadequate. It also struck me that delivering advice to my patients was a lot easier than giving myself advice about how to act.

We waited. It felt like hours. She finally returned, high and scared. It seemed that the "new friend" had introduced her to oxycodone, also known as Hillbilly Heroin or Blues. I kept pushing her for more information and she pushed back. I was trying to understand the extent of her problem and she was trying to ascertain what the police had told us.

My wife began to cry. It wasn't a bad idea. But, I controlled myself and pressed on. We were just as scared as she was. She was, at that time, still new enough to the disease to almost care about what we thought.

The advice I gave to parents that came to the pharmacy was that shouting would accomplish nothing. I therefore breathed deeply and tried to speak civilly but we were getting nowhere. I caught myself getting stern and quickly retreated. Our daughter retired to her room.

We could not just let this drop. We were lucky to have gotten a warning. If we did nothing, we would never be able to forgive ourselves if something happened to her. We had to get help. All we could think was, "There must be *someone* who could help us." I realized that at this time it was up to me to take control of the situation. My wife loves the children but I am the parent. My wife prefers to be a friend to the children with certain exceptions and I am the disciplinarian. So I sat and thought.

Stay Cool
But Get Help

"Don't get crazy with your child, but you must deal with it."
"You must get help for them."

"Shouting does nothing but sends them on a run—makes them tune out and leave to use."

These were all things I had said to parents at the pharmacy, never knowing I would have to take my own advice one day.

Although most kids often return home after a few hours (especially in the early stages of addiction) there is a tendency for them to isolate when your reaction is to shout and make a scene. I knew this logically. But now the problem had hit home. It was now a personal issue and like the doctor who cannot objectively treat their own family member, I too knew not what to do. I was emotionally crippled.

Eventually, we decided to call a great friend who was a judge in the Drug Court. She was very sympathetic. I saw addicts coming into the pharmacy, trying to get their prescriptions filled. She saw those same addicts…after they had been arrested. She told us that the most important thing to do was not to lose our tempers or shout and to calmly discuss what was happening to get our daughter to agree to enter into treatment. She explained that there were many facilities out there but not all were equal. She offered to make a few calls and get back to us. I could only feel numbness and thankfulness—numbness over the current situation and thankfulness for the help I was about to receive.

Good friends are hard to come by, but I always prided myself on being a sincere and helpful person to all whether they were patients, friends, strangers, or family. This had often been mistaken for me being "easy" but if easy is being nice to people then I guess I am. It was time to see if my niceness had been taken for granted or accepted for what it was and so far the response seemed to be in my favor. It felt good to know I had a friend. The judge called back shortly thereafter and told me of a few places that were "better than average treatment centers" but if she had to send a family member to any one in particular, one stood out. She had spoken to the owner who said we should call him as soon as possible as his place was small and they were often full. I thanked her from the heart and could only hope that she knew how much that she had helped. We finally had a plan.

I spoke with Z in her room. I was calm but forceful. I told her that with my limited knowledge of the disease, I knew that she had a problem and it had to be treated. Amazingly, she agreed to go. One never knows what an addict is thinking as their thought process is distorted—you don't know if they are agreeing with you because they think you're right, or because they have never been through the process of rehab before and want to experience something new, or perhaps they just need a break from the drug life, and this is a way to clean house and have the insurance company pay for it. Whatever the reason, I accepted her agreement and told her I would update her when I knew more details.

What I didn't know at this time was that, while getting your addicted loved one into treatment is important—there is no guarantee that it will be successful. The odds are increased if the desire to enter into treatment *comes from the one suffering from the disease.* This is a two-phase deal. The first is physical—the detoxification portion of treatment. Your loved one is assessed by a specialist in the field of detoxification who prescribes a program for their detoxification from the drug or drugs they are addicted to. Upon completion of the detoxification process, they then enter into phase two: the treatment portion. This occurs if they have reached a point whereby they are capable of comprehending what a therapist is trying to accomplish with them. Depending on what drugs they're addicted to and how long they have used for, some may require a more prolonged time in the detox phase of treatment.

This is a disease that has been maligned for many years and until just recently, most saw drug abuse/addiction as something done by criminals when in fact, it is one of the most complicated diseases that a therapist will encounter, regardless of a patient's socio-economic background. Many therapists specializing in addiction leave the field due to the frustration—repeatedly trying to treat the same patients suffering from this disease can be exhausting. This fact further illustrates that your loved one's actions do not reflect *their emotions or feelings toward you*. You should never feel guilt—you have *not caused* this.

I called the treatment center and made arrangements to bring my daughter in the following morning. That night was a restless one. The thought that she had a drug problem was enough to keep me up—but the fear that perhaps she might sneak out of the house and disappear before she got help was worse. The night crept along slowly but I must have dozed off eventually as suddenly it was 6 am and I was awake. My wife was already making coffee. Z packed enough things for at least a month. She conscientiously asked about notifying her employer and I told her that we would ask for guidance about that at the center. Too soon, it seemed, we were driving to the treatment center.

The owner, Joe, personally greeted us and while Z was taken to a room to undergo the process of entry, we were given a little insight as to what lay ahead of us. Joe had a segregated facility, meaning that while men and women were treated there, they lived and were treated separately. He told us that one night a week there was a Family Night and invited us to attend the next one. He told us we were about to enter into a new world of which we knew nothing, and explained that the best way to assist Z in her journey along the road to sobriety was to learn as much about the disease of addiction as possible; to do this we, like the addict, should also attend meetings.

As treatment centers can get overwhelmed, they sometimes forget that the parents or family members are scared, too. In the case of a husband or wife perhaps scared is not what they are feeling. They may be suffering from a variety of emotions ranging from anxiety and confusion about what is going on to a feeling of doom brought on by thoughts of their marriage being on the verge of destruction. At this time, a few words of compassion and support from the admissions personnel may be something beyond thoughtfulness. This is especially true if this is the first admission for the client. If the person working with you seems unempathetic towards you please don't hesitate to ask questions as they should be there to assist you as long as there is no violation of the HIPPA law (that's the Health Insurance Portability and Accountability Act of 1996, a federal law designed to protect sensitive patient health information from being disclosed without the patient's consent or knowledge). Should they act nasty or indifferent, ask to speak to someone else. Remember, this is a family disease and they should show you as much courtesy as they do the client. What my wife and I have endured is not unique.

He then brought us back to where Z was—sitting at a desk with a counselor. He greeted us with a smile, trying to set us parents at ease, knowing that this was as scary for us as it surely must have been for our daughter since this was her first entry into treatment. This had an effect on us that is hard to explain: it's kind of an empty sensation that consists of shame, guilt, and a hollowness that can only be explained as despair.

Z said she wanted to tell him something personal so the therapist asked us to leave for a moment. I was puzzled by this but was told that there was total confidentiality and that the patient's anonymity was protected except for what may be brought out at Family Night. Ruefully, I smiled inwardly at my conception of what treatment was like and my lack of knowledge as to the extent of my daughter's addiction. When we were asked to return, we were told what the future held for her in the facility and then were shocked to hear that she would first be sent to a detoxification center (better known as Detox) where she would be safe while her body withdrew from the drugs that she was addicted to. "Drugs," we noticed—just how many was she addicted to? We'd never know unless she decided to tell us herself or gave them permission (usually written) to discuss her situation with us.

Z excused herself, asking where the ladies' room was. When she sat back down with us, the session resumed. I asked when she would leave for the Detox center and was told that the facility was sending a van to pick her up as soon as possible. I sensed that the meeting was over and we got up to leave. The counselor who ran the programs (for both the male and female sides) then led us to a waiting area. Whether it was because of my friend, the judge, we'll never know, but he waited with us.

It was then that I began to notice that my daughter was not as coherent as she had been and she was staggering around. Obviously, she had smuggled some drugs in with her, thus the sudden urge to use the bathroom. I told my wife that our daughter was stoned out of her head. She walked over to Z and spoke to her in a soft tone. She told me that Z replied that she seemed stoned because she was "beginning to withdraw from the drugs" and to "stop picking on her."

I whispered to my wife that if bullshit were a commodity, the kid would be rich. My wife was upset with me. I turned to the counselor, who smiled, and asked him where she could have gotten the drugs from. He replied that most clients entering into treatment brought or found drugs to take that "last splurge" before entering into the sober world known as treatment. He assured us that once she reached the Detox center they would search her and her possessions for anything that she shouldn't have. My wife learned a lesson at that moment: the addict's mind is cunning. If only the effort they expended trying to get high were steered toward constructive paths, they could be very successful entrepreneurs.

After what seemed like an eternity, the van pulled up. The driver got out, approached the counselor, and was handed some paperwork. He then supported my staggering daughter the short distance to the van, and off they went. You have at this time, very mixed emotions. On the one hand, you feel relief. Your daughter is on the path to becoming well. On the other hand, the shame and guilt you feel is overwhelming. This is the beginning of either what could be a hell, or a onetime trip. You, as the parent of an addict in treatment for the first time, do not know this yet, but the odds are not in their favor. Two feelings that the family members of an addict are entitled to at this point are hope and shame. The hope should never leave. The shame should. Sometimes the shame is replaced with despair. As a therapist friend who worked at the rehab explained it, *compassion fatigue* can set in, but one should never let this consume them. One should never give up hope. Thankfully there are people out there who are willing to help. If your loved one is still alive *there is always hope*.

There are many facilities out there that will help you with your family member. Some are good, some are not so good, and some are just plain *bad*. As with any healthcare facility, some care and devote themselves to patients, and some are in the business to make a fast buck. Unfortunately looking at their website doesn't tell you which facilities are good or bad. I never once saw a site that claimed that the facility was in the business for the money. There are, however many such facilities. Sometimes the addict enters a facility to eat, have a place to sleep, get their family off their back, and get back on the street fast (all at the insurance company's expense) so they are not always the best source of information. The more practical way to find a place is to speak with family members or someone who has straight time who really cares.

Many family members of addicts have had the experience of their loved one going in and out of treatment. After several treatment centers, they begin to develop a sense of which centers care and which don't. The same may be true with someone suffering from the disease. They often have been to many facilities before entering into long-term sobriety. They are usually helpful in selecting which facility is a good one. Remember, no facility is a good one if the client doesn't want help.

Don't be scared by stories of frequent relapse. These are true. They are part of the disease. Never give up hope as you never know which treatment is the one that gives you back your loved one. Remember, a good facility can only be as good as the client will allow it to be.

The Rehab Process

Z entered into Detox and we went home. We didn't know how to feel—or where her Detox center was—and my wife was crying. For the first few days we heard nothing. There was a kind of void in our lives. Up until the call from the police, we lived what we thought to be fairly normal lives at home; now we actually missed the moaning and bitching that Z had brought into the house. My wife was in a constant state of worry since this was the first time she'd felt that everything was out of her control. It's funny how the mind adjusts to different situations. It goes something like this: You have an addict living at home. Perhaps due to your unwillingness to see it, or your brain becoming conditioned to a set of circumstances that you have lived with for a certain period of time, a defense mechanism kicks in and you *phased out what you were seeing*. You begin to realize that your awareness of the severity of the situation has never entered into your reality. *Is my daughter really an addict? Was I so blind to her actions?*

It's a slow metamorphosis from a normal teen to a young adult suffering from a disease. Suddenly you're dropped into a pool of ice water and due to hindsight, you see all the signs that you did not or would not see before and you start to blame yourself.

We couldn't even visit Z until the following week. The waiting was painful. I assured my wife that if something bad had happened we would have been notified. As the saying goes, "no news is good news." To deal with her anxiety, my wife cleaned the house constantly.

As discussed with the facility owner, we prepared to attend Family Night. Due to my schedule, I was only able to make the men's meeting that week. The owner assured us that this too would be a learning experience and the most important thing to do at this time was to learn as much as possible about the disease. Z would be in the Detox center anyway, so we could not yet see her.

Wednesday night we went with mixed emotions to our first Family Night. We knew nothing about what would happen or what a meeting was like. We were both anxious to learn and embarrassed that this could happen to our family. When we arrived at the center, there were chairs neatly arranged for both the family members and clients. (I quickly found out the patients are referred to as "clients.") There were several other parents there, both from the area and out of town. Soon the bus pulled up, the clients disembarked, and the room was suddenly full. I recognized the owner sitting at the table in front as the meeting was called to order. The clients and family members introduced themselves. I was glad I was sitting towards the rear so that I could familiarize myself with the proper manner of introduction. I would later find out that this did not matter as introductions become informal and with familiarity comes a bonding very similar to the bonds between family members.

It is better to listen and learn rather than give an uninformed opinion, so I sat and listened. The stories were frank and scary. Some parents were scared and upset and couldn't understand why their family members were unable to get and stay straight. Others were totally burned out and wanted to give up on the person. They were still there, so there must have been some feelings left. This could not be the world into which my daughter had entered. Surely *she was different* and once she completed treatment, she would begin her life over again. What I was hearing was clearly only true of these others.

First, these were *guys* and she was my daughter *the honor student*. Second, true she had screwed up, but hadn't she just partied too hard, taking "a few pills too many?" Soon this would be over with her having learned a good lesson. We sat and listened to the other family members speak. Their stories were heartbreaking but had *nothing to do with our daughter*.

I did, however, find the meeting passionate and exciting and vowed to learn as much as I could about addiction. I would make arrangements to be off Tuesday nights so that I could attend the ladies' night as well as the men's. I figured that if one meeting was good, two would be twice as good. Aha, I figured something right. After the meeting my wife and I went to the desk where the owner was mobbed by parents and family members wanting to ask questions.

We started to speak with a client's mother who was at her wit's end as this was her son's fifth trip to treatment. She asked if this was our first trip and we nodded. She smiled and told us to get ready for the roller-coaster ride of a lifetime. We spoke for a few minutes, thinking to ourselves that she didn't know anything. This would be the *one and only trip* for our daughter. I began to get a niggling feeling by the end of the night: *what if this woman was right? Was there a possibility of relapse for Z in the future?*

The ride home was long and silent. Our lack of understanding of the disease caused unexplainable feelings. I was determined to learn everything about this disease so I could beat these odd new emotions. How complicated could it be? *After all, I'm a pharmacist.* I took all those chemistry and biology courses. I should be able to learn this stuff in no time at all.

My next day off I took a trip to the local bookstore and found the section on addiction. I soon found one that was right up my alley, *The Complete Idiot's Guide-Substance Abuse* I found it interesting, but more important, I began to notice that the more I read, the more there was to know. Whoever wrote it was certainly no idiot. The more I read, the more I began to analyze what was being said. This was indeed a very complex disease that people not affiliated with it will ever comprehend, just like only the addict can appreciate the strength of the urge to use. Unlike most diseases the patient does not (at first) appear sick. Reading about addiction is a way to try to understand, but only through experience can someone really learn. This is not to mean that you should go out and get high, but rather you should attend meetings and listen to what families say as they have been through what you are just entering into. The meetings may be an inconvenience, but they are important if you want to gain the knowledge and the perspective needed to deal with this disease.

After a few days of hearing nothing, the phone rang. It was Z. She assured us that she was okay and that on Sunday afternoon we could come to the Detox center and visit. As big a pain in the ass as she could be, we missed her dearly. As Sunday approached, our excitement grew. We could not wait to visit her and see the center. The Rehab center was not too impressive so we were hoping that the Detox center looked better. When you see the commercials, you always see these glamorous facilities, where they give you massages and put hot rocks on your back, and you assume they will all look like this. I would soon find out that it is not what the facility looks like, but rather the dedication and determination on the part of the staff and the client that is what determines how successfully the treatment may turn out.

Sunday finally arrived and after one of the longest mornings we had experienced, it was time to leave. We got into the car feeling both excited and depressed. Excited, because we couldn't wait to see our new daughter, and depressed because you never lose the feeling that this *could not really be happening* to your family member. The trip took longer than expected or at least it felt that way. We spoke very little. We hoped to find her in good spirits and well.

To say that we were a little disappointed with the appearance of the facility when we arrived would have to be an understatement. It appeared to be clean, but the building was basically a dump. We entered and were greeted by the administrator. He checked the packages that we had brought for her to make sure we weren't sneaking in anything that wasn't permitted and then told us that although she was doing well, she still had not completed the detoxification process but that she would be returned to the treatment center by the end of seven days as that was the maximum that insurance covered. He assured us that the facility that she was to return to was more than adequately capable of taking her through the residual effects of detoxification.

We entered the client area and there was our daughter, waiting for us to arrive. Though she was sitting with others, she looked alone and scared and our hearts broke as we went to her. She stood up when she saw us and smiled. There was our daughter again.

We walked outside together into the backyard and found a place to sit and speak about her treatment.

My wife was a little lost but I of course knew about the drugs used to detoxify the addict. I was pretty sure that she was coming off the opiates with the aid of Suboxone, a drug that both blocks the action of the opiate as well as supplies a substitute so that the client does not enter into a severe withdrawal. There was also the possibility that they had her on a non-addicting anti-anxiety agent such as Seroquel to keep her agitation at a minimum. That would be my educated guess as I was never told if she had abused any other drugs. She was a little tense when we spoke about her leaving Detox as she felt that perhaps she needed more time with the detoxification process. I assured her that the facility was capable of making that judgment and if they felt that she needed more time, she would get it. She accepted this and we had a fairly good visit. She told us that the food was excellent (when she could eat it) and although the place looked like a dump it was actually quite nice. This set our mind at ease, especially my wife's, who cleaned the house daily. I totally expected her to ask if she could change the linen in my daughter's room.

After several hours we felt that it was time to leave. We hugged and kissed Z and said our goodbyes to the administrator. The ride home was solemn. My wife was not happy with the appearance of the facility. She kept saying it looked dirty and old and was located in the dumpy section of town. She said the place looked like there were pushers around the neighborhood. I could not help but feel that perhaps there was some truth to what she was saying. To cheer up, we went out to dinner. It was good, but we couldn't get our child out of our minds.

Monday morning I called the owner of the rehab center and spoke with him about our concerns. He is a wonderful man who understood how we felt and assured us that he had sent her to one of the finest Detox facilities in the state. He told us that although we hear about the war on drugs and how concerned the populace is with the addiction epidemic, *nobody* wants the facilities in *their* neighborhood, so unless the owner is a celebrity with a lot of powerful friends, the centers are kind of restricted to the not-so-great areas. He then told us it is not the appearance but rather how they are run that counts and to relax as while she was interned we did not have to worry about where she was or what she was doing. He also told us to enjoy life when we could as far too soon she would be completing the process and then the time for concern begins again. I thanked him, hung up and called my wife to relay the conversation. I smiled to myself, feeling at ease. I hoped my wife felt the same, but there was no way to tell until that night after work when I returned home. (Work helps take one's mind off of their problems.)

Finally Tuesday arrived and we prepared to go to the Family Night meeting for women. We entered a room on the other side of the facility and were greeted by the therapist. She spoke with us and to our surprise, Z had arrived that day and we would get to see her. The therapist had a way of asking questions that made us aware that her job was to try to figure out what had led to Z's addiction. This was both reassuring and scary as most addict's family members are convinced that the blame rests squarely upon their shoulders.

We looked for a seat where we could not be seen. Unfortunately (or fortunately?), there was nowhere to hide. We found two seats; we spoke with the therapist for a few minutes and soon others began to arrive. The facility was available to clients and family members as well as alumni and the family members of the alumni, whether or not they came or were still in treatment. The alumni go to the meetings to learn and to receive help, as well as to give input to those who are new and going through the inpatient process for the first time.

My wife asked me what to do if the therapist asked her questions. I told her that it would be best to answer the question as honestly and objectively as possible. There would be no right or wrong answers as this was not a test. She relaxed a little. The room was filling up and suddenly there was Z. She saw us and smiled but looked a little ill. She asked my wife if she could bring some toiletries to the next week's meeting for her. We made a list of things to bring.

The therapist called the meeting to order and those standing sat, and the room quieted down. Thankfully, our seats were not located next to the therapist as the room was crowded and even with my speaking experience, I felt like everyone was watching me as I introduced myself as Z's father and said that the purpose of my attendance was to learn and to support her. I sat there, wondering how this could have happened. The shame was overwhelming. I was sure that everyone was looking at us. What a strange feeling as I had often told patients in my pharmacy who had come to speak with me upon finding that their child might have a drug problem that there was "no need for shame as this was a disease." True objectivity comes into question when one is involved on a personal level.

The therapist had piercing eyes as she scanned the room looking for someone to speak with. She must have seen the look of terror on our faces and so passed us by and began to question a client. I found it amazing how this woman seemed to know that the client was having a problem just by reading her facial expression. She spoke with her for about a half hour, digging deeper and deeper into the cause of her anxiety and as the discussion ended she opened the floor up for input from the other people in the room.

Someone very wise once gave me advice that I still follow. He told me that if I don't know what I'm talking about, I shouldn't talk and that listening is how people learn. Learning is how you become capable of speaking intelligently. So with this bit of knowledge stored away in my mind I quietly sat and listened, feeling more and more confident that perhaps the therapist knew my wise friend too, and would let me gain some knowledge before questioning my family.

Soon the break came and we rose and walked around while my daughter went out with the other clients to smoke a cigarette. This was something that she had only begun since entering treatment. She had never smoked before and I was surprised that she had started at this late age. With all her other addictions I figured that this was not the time to preach about the negatives of smoking. This was something I hoped she would stop after her release from treatment.

During the break we met with other parents and spoke a little. They seemed nice and they too had that look upon their face—that they were sick inside at the thought of having an addicted child. Those that lived within traveling distance said they came to every meeting and that they felt this was important as it was both a source of knowledge and a show of support which they felt was a necessary part of treatment. I did notice that there were more clients than family members so I could only conclude that this meant that either they were from out of town or their loved ones were no longer loved ones. After the break we returned to our seats and once again we were filled with anxiety, waiting to see if we would be called upon and questioned. We waited, listened, and finally the time was up. The meeting ended and my wife and I were relieved that we had not been picked out to be analyzed. We drove home, determined to return the following Tuesday.

The one thing that had imprinted upon my mind was that this was the time to relax as while Z was in rehab, she was safe. There was no worry of her overdosing or getting arrested or into an accident. She was in a protected environment with constant supervision. So this, for family members, is the time to live our lives perhaps a little more comfortably, for however short a period of time it is. We must also assume that our loved ones aren't going to choose to walk out and relapse. This however, is not the norm. Occasionally, a resident will relapse and leave but for the most part while in treatment the clients are conscientious. We still had the thought that most first-timers have, that like most diseases, that after treatment she would be cured. How naïve we were.

We continued to attend the weekly Tuesday night meetings. I listened intently. First, the meetings were interesting. Second, and most importantly, I would try to analyze all that was going on to learn about this insidious disease. There are three main ways to gain knowledge: visually, auditorily, and kinetically. Or more simply put: watch, listen, partake. Never be ashamed to ask questions. Despite visuals of criminals and thugs, addicts who have completed Detox and entered Rehab are surprisingly pleasant and openly attentive to the program of recovery—not to mention extremely repentant.

With few exceptions, the clients would often be reduced to tears as they were asked to tell what their life was like while in active addiction. I remember one client who was asked to share in a session. She seemed to be all right initially as she told of how she and her friends would party on the weekends smoking weed and listening to music and then they would walk to the diner and load up on fries and other snacks. She then told how she met this boy who turned her on to a Blue (slang for an oxycodone tablet). At first she was scared, but the effect was so nice that she later told her friends about it and they too tried it and soon they were partying with Blues instead of weed. The fear that she had initially felt from the jump from marijuana to oxycodone soon faded as she figured it was "only a 'weekend thing' so the chance of getting addicted was none." She spoke about how nice it made her feel. Her friends loved the feeling, too.

Soon they were using on a more frequent basis and it didn't take long before she realized that if she didn't take one she would get sick. She would get cramps, diarrhea, and aches so she used more and more. It was an expensive affair that she had gotten herself into and she was scared. She was scared because she was losing control and scared because she felt that she couldn't talk to her parents about her situation. She graduated high school and went away to college. Before she left her parents threw her a going away party and some of her family gave her money to have for a good time at college. She used some of this money to see a doctor her friends told her about and got a supply of oxycodone to hold her for a while.

It was at college that she met a guy that told her that she was nuts for using Blues as they cost a fortune. He used to do that but now used heroin. It was much cheaper and he kept a lid on how he used it. He would wait until he was sick to use again so he didn't use that much. She tried it. The high was nicer and the price was cheaper. "What the hell, I'm hooked anyway" was her thinking. This went on for a few months. She and her boyfriend hung out with a group of students that all used. She was using daily. She flunked out of school and moved back home. She told her mother she was looking for a job but was getting high instead. She needed money, so she would go through her mother's jewelry to look for things she didn't use any more and sold them. Her mother figured out what was happening and her choice was to get treatment or get out. She left.

She moved in with a friend and hustled for money. She would shoplift primarily. It was easy to just pick something up at a chain store, go to customer service, and tell them she wanted to return it but didn't have the receipt. They would give her a money card. Then she would go outside, sell it for half price, and then buy a bag of heroin. In between loads she said she did feel guilty about what she was doing but the next shot took care of that. Eventually she got arrested and got released. After this happened a few times, she was given the choice: she could either go into treatment or head to jail. She went home and spoke to her parents. They found this place and so here she was. She cried. She cried for what she put her parents through. She cried for what she did to herself. She swore this was the end. This is not a unique story. As a matter of fact, it is the rule, not the exception. Most people that suffer from this relapse after their first time. There are always exceptions to this statement but hopefully your loved one does not fall into this category. Hopefully they make it. There are "one-time wonders," as they are referred to. I do know that their chances of success are increased if they know they have your support.

Each week would bring new clients and sometimes new families, as it was not always possible for the client's families to attend for various reasons. Some clients came from out of town. Others had caused such destruction within their family structure that they would have to work hard to regain the bonds that had once existed. I believe that the family never loses the love they have for a child. I know that my wife and I have never given up on our daughter, although we have set boundaries that we feel are vital to our survival. These boundaries have nothing to do with the love we have for her. What she has done is common. It is part of the actions and the survival mechanism for those in active addiction. I speak to the late-night calls from the police, the hospital calling about the overdose. The missing items that can be sold so that they can buy drugs. These are the things that we have to live with and what the addict feels that we have broken trust with them about. The fact is the addict feels that once we react to this situation;

perhaps by asking them to leave home, that we no longer feel a connection with them. This of course is not to be taken as the entire population, but a large percentage of those that are asked to leave the house by family believe that they are no longer welcome by their family. They don't understand us, just as we don't understand them. The intensity of the destructiveness of this disease can be overwhelming. It can take a loving family member and change them into a totally different person—this goes for both the addict and the family. Keep in mind that this is a family disease: it can destroy not only the addict's life, but the family members' as well. I try to explain to the client that the break most likely can be mended as there is a prolongation of recovery but this is not an easy task as an addict in early recovery is still not totally thinking rationally and the therapist plays a major part here by connecting the two with a simple phone call.

As I continued to learn about the disease, I began to understand the meaning of the *Dr. Jekyll and Mr. Hyde* syndrome. But always, there lingered the thought that *this could not be my daughter*. She was always so nice at home, had a great sense of humor, and was often the perfect child. Surely she was the exception. After all, she just got "caught up" in that pill mill mess and partied too hardy. A few bad choices could not turn my daughter into an addict. By now she must have surely learned her lesson. This place was good for her. It would show her how you can end up if you *really* become an addict. *My darling daughter, I hope you are learning as much as I am trying to learn. The road you almost went down is the road to hell and it seems the road back is a long and hard one—much more complicated than the road leading to addiction. Thank God that the police officer alerted us to what was going on before it was too late.*

The four weeks passed quickly. Each week she would request more items for us to bring her. I would ask my wife why she needed all of this stuff. I wondered if she was playing a game. "Bring me more clean clothes and Mom can wash them all when I get home." I ran this by my wife and she said she didn't care. I couldn't help but feel that needing all of these clothes and cosmetics might perhaps *be a part* of the problem. I was, however, a novice and felt that the counselors would intervene if they saw something that was contrary to policy. This did not occur so I continued to bring clothes and makeup each week until I thought that I would have to rent a truck to bring her things home when she was released.

Codependency, what we both were guilty of, is a major problem that is entwined with this disease. What is it? This is a good question to which there is actually no single answer. There are books on this concept that try to explain it, but like this disease, it is complicated. I like to tell families that if you are doing something for your loved one *that they should be doing for themselves* then you are being codependent. For example, "My daughter is going to need her car to get to work when she finds a better job so for now I will make her car payment." Or, "If she doesn't pay her insurance, her coverage will lapse and her driver's license will be suspended so I have to make her payment for her so when she stops using she can drive to the job that she will get."

The recommended way to stop the codependency process is *to set and maintain boundaries* (another concept that is often easier said than done). The concept of boundaries evolves as compassion fatigue progresses. The therapist tells you that you must set boundaries and that you have to *stop* doing the thing for your loved one that they should be doing for themselves. But, it has been my experience that this is easier said than done. As your loved one burns you a few times and you realize that nice is not nice and you have been used as the *addict is using the money they are saving via the money you are spending to help them*, to buy drugs. This is a learning process that takes time and it hurts. For this reason, don't blame yourself for doing the wrong thing. Rather, try to learn from others' experiences.

The Family Night meetings were the best part of my journey toward gaining insight into this very mysterious world. Each Tuesday we would drive to the center and listen to the therapist as she went about trying to make the family understand their miscomprehensions about the disease, and make the client reveal what was disturbing about their life. My wife would sit there, hoping she would not get called upon and I would sit there, trying to devour all the knowledge that I could. It was all very confusing to me. One week I would think that I understood something, only to discover that what I thought was right was wrong the next week.

Would I ever get this disease figured out? As a pharmacist, I figured that science is physical. This drug treats this and that drug treats that. Barring any side effects, you use the drug and the symptoms go away. This disease was not anywhere near that concept, and it would take me a long time to figure out the basics. You will find that generally, the therapist will helpfully guide you so that your idea will come across in a more tactful and acceptable manner to others in the event that you might be speaking from a place of frustration or anger. Never be ashamed to ask questions as this too is how you will learn about this disease. You will find that as your knowledge begins to take hold so will your confidence to partake in the discussions. Families, and especially the therapist, will guide the discussion and correct any misconceptions. Often your input will be vindictive. Although this is something to try to avoid, it's going to happen and can be attributed to the negative experiences that you have been put through by your loved one.

Keep in mind, at this point in their recovery, the client is usually remorseful for all that they have done to their family and loved ones. They will be more receptive to the negative input as they too are in a learning process, especially those who are new to treatment. But as they gain knowledge and self-esteem they will probably develop hostility towards this vitriol as they too have a point of view which just might hold their family's actions in a negative perspective.

Yes, there is often conflict between the client and their families. This occurs for many reasons. The greatest reason is that as sobriety progresses so does one's self esteem and this gives the client a more positive feeling about what their sense of right is. For example, they may claim that they were never allowed to emotionally mature as their parents refused to allow them to do what someone their age should be doing. For instance, paying their own rent or making their own car payments. The parents may counter that the client was too stoned to do these things. Perhaps the therapist may chime in that maybe they were too stoned because they had no responsibilities. Family Night is the place for these feelings to be released. All things said, the clients are usually very happy to have these interactions with their loved ones and there are hugs at the end of the night.

We were very optimistic about the outcome of this stay. About halfway through the treatment process (that lasted approximately a month) Z was given a weekend pass to come home. This was based upon good behavior but I got the feeling that if you lived locally and asked for permission it would be granted—as long as they didn't catch you sneaking out the window in the middle of the night, you received permission to have a home visit. I made arrangements to be off that weekend so that I could pick her up and spend some quality time with her. She had not slept in her own bed for over three weeks and I was sure she would be happy to be home.

The week went by slowly. Finally, after what seemed like another three weeks had passed, Saturday arrived and my wife and I drove to the facility to pick Z up. A technician was waiting to discuss the procedure with us: she was not to go out at night on her own, she should make every effort to attend either an AA or NA meeting Saturday and Sunday, she had to be back at the treatment center by 5 pm Sunday, and if she brought anything back with her it must be brought to the technician on duty for inspection. We agreed to everything and drove off.

Home was nice. Our family was back together. Her sisters, who lived nearby, came to see how she was doing. She seemed like a different person. Once again, she was smiling and acted like the daughter of past times. It seemed as though sobriety agreed with her. Life was once again well…perhaps too well. There had been too much talk during Family Nights at the center about deception, manipulation, and relapse for a paranoid person like myself to be totally at ease.

We relaxed and spoke about what we should have for dinner. Anything was on the table as this was a celebration. We decided to go out for seafood and thoroughly enjoyed the meal; especially not having to argue about not ordering alcoholic beverages. After we returned home, I suggested that we go to a meeting. Z replied that it was late and that she was tired. She said that she went to meetings every night at the center and needed a break. This sounded reasonable to me so I agreed to wait until Sunday.

Sunday morning after we went out for breakfast, Z came out of the computer room claiming that we had missed a morning meeting and would have to wait until the evening. I reminded her that she had to be back by 5 pm. She said that that was perfect. She would shower before we left so that she could attend the meeting with the other clients. I felt a little put out as some of the parents mentioned that they sometimes attended meetings with their children. They claimed it helped them bond (and they therefore *knew* that their child went to the meeting). I did not complain as confidentiality is a part of this disease and perhaps she didn't want me to hear what she had to say. I was too new to the disease to know if I was being manipulated or if we were guilty of poor planning. You hear so much about the addict's ability to manipulate people that you don't know what to think. We were told to make a meeting—*at least one*—while she was at home, and we hadn't. Was this my fault or hers? Probably the smartest thing to do was to let the technician know that she missed the meetings and perhaps, as she said she would, she could make the Sunday night meeting.

At Family Night it was our time to speak with the therapist. She asked Z how it had been to be home. I assumed that this would be friendly chatter and she would quickly move on to one of the new clients. Eventually, the therapist began asking slightly more complex questions about how close Z was with her mother. When she asked if Z had done laundry at home, my wife replied that she had done it for her. There were several other things that were brought up such as, "Did Z prepare her own breakfast?"

I felt this to be unfair because she was home on a visit and we wanted to treat her well so we went out to eat our meals. I never realized the significance, at that time, of my daughter doing those things for herself. The therapist was both congenial and firm. She didn't just tell us that we should have had Z do more (and have attended at least one meeting), she also explained to us why this was important. She intimated that perhaps Z had played us like a fiddle. Though she resented that accusation, Z protested little.

On the way home, my wife was annoyed. She is a dominant person and resented being told how to behave with Z. I, on the other hand, felt that if something was broken there was a reason for the break. She *resented*, I tried to *learn*—a definite schism in our thinking processes. I am by nature a quiet soft-spoken type. I was taught to "say what you know and know what you say." At this point I knew that the therapists knew substantially more than I and therefore left the care of Z in their hands. They were the professionals, this was a disease, and just as I would not tell my cardiologist how to treat a heart attack, I now felt that I should not tell the therapists how to treat our daughter.

However, the process of educating yourself includes the act of questioning the actions which you are not sure of. You will find that as you become more acquainted with this disease you might find yourself questioning what the therapist is saying and if you ask why, you should get an answer. Often therapists disagree in their approaches toward the disease. This is because it is not an exact science with an exact approach toward reaching recovery. Often a group of therapists working with a patient will discuss their approaches and one may change their method or they just might agree that the different methods are a mitigating process towards recovery. For instance one therapist may prefer to use a direct method of treatment. They might ask the client why they reacted in a violet manner to the question asked. Another therapist might prefer an experiential approach where two clients talk to each other to try to get the client to open up as to what was buried deep inside them that brought out the hostility.

Sometimes, two therapists just might disagree on a principle. An example of this is one therapist disagrees with me when I say that when an addict is in the state of active addiction it is harder on the family than on the addict, who at that time has the ability to hide their emotions by getting high. So there is one therapist that I feel is defensive when someone speaks in a negative manner about those that suffer from the disease of addiction. This could be due to the fact that she has a son that suffers from the disease.

It is often said that the addicted are cunning and manipulative. I stated this and she got upset, asking why people felt it necessary to defame those that suffer from the disease of addiction. I replied that I was not defaming them; rather I was pointing out a symptom of the disease. She wouldn't accept my explanation, so I proceeded to ask the group: when they were in active addiction and were entering into withdrawal, what would they do? They would "score some dope." I then asked "If you had no money, what would you do?" The answer was, "I would still score some dope!"

"Without money how would you do this?" The answer was, "We would find a way."

"To accomplish this, would you have to develop skill that could be considered cunning or manipulative?" The answer was, "Yes." The therapist then asked, "Would you consider this a part of your survival skills?" Again, the answer was yes. So, as a father who perhaps is closer to reaching compassion fatigue than the therapist, we have two different outlooks. Both of our opinions were right.

The wonderful thing about Family Night is that you can discuss an issue with the therapist who then tries to work it out with the help of the other families who are going through the same (or close to the same) situation that you are going through. I found out that if not resolved, a situation could be brought back to the center where it could be worked on later that week. You were not looked down upon should you say something that could be adversely construed but rather the group would work it so that you left understanding why what you thought was incorrect. That is, if you are open to the input. If that is the case, it might take some time before you would allow yourself to accept the input that the group has to offer.

At one meeting there was a new client whose parents had come to learn about the disease and give support. It was a heavy first meeting for them as the mother was convinced that the daughter's addiction was a result of something that she had done. The therapist began by speaking to the client, her daughter. She asked what it was that her mother had done to drive her to use drugs. The daughter, who had gone through the detox process and already attended one family night without her parents being present (something that is sometimes dome so that the client can be further along in the detoxification process and therefore more rational in their behavior), responded that her parents were wonderful and loving and nothing to do with her addiction. The therapist turned to the mother and asked why she believed that her child's addiction was her fault. The mother responded that this doesn't just happen so she must have done something wrong. The therapist worked on this for about a half hour and then turned to the next client. The following week, the mother again began to cry, stating, "It had to be something that I did to cause this disease." This continued throughout the client's stay. No matter what the client shared, what the other parents said, or what the therapist tried to do with the mother, she would not accept the premise that she could not have caused her daughter to enter into the disease of addiction.

Z was either a good patient or knew how to work the system for she was permitted to come home on weekend passes for remainder of her time in the program. This she liked and I must admit so did mom and pop. It was nice to have the family together again. *Soon she will complete the program and come home cured.* Alas, that there is a cure for this disease is a thought that belongs to those who have no knowledge of addiction for *there is no cure* for this disease. At this time, the cure is often referred to as death—no joke. Just as diabetes has no cure, the disease of addiction has no cure. There is remission. The term used for remission is "recovery" and the state of being in recovery is as close to a cure as one can get.

On the weekends we would pick her up, take her home, and enjoy our time together. She was a new person. She spoke like an adult, acted like an adult, and even pointed people out to us who were high. I was so proud of her. I couldn't wait for her to return to work and start attending nightly meetings. I planned to have a celebration at home every time she got a new chip. A chip is part of a system that the 12-step fellowships use to encourage sobriety. A chip or token—be it a disc or keychain—is awarded to the person in recovery at certain intervals such as every three months until they reach a year. Then they are awarded on a yearly basis. I failed to notice that perhaps I was little more enthusiastic about the tokens and parties than she was.

Finally, we were called by the therapy director and told to come in, as Z was to be released soon and a meeting with the therapist was part of the end of the program. The client's therapist meets with the client and family to discuss the progress made and different programs that the client should partake in after release to aid in maintaining their sobriety. We arrived early and sat in the reception area until the therapist emerged from her office and brought us in. Z was then brought in and we discussed several positive areas she had excelled in and then some that they thought required more time in therapy. I felt that she was wrong. Z would be back at work in no time and that would be the best therapy. I told her that when we were home I would talk with Z about outpatient therapy. She had been, after all, out of work and on disability for over a month. Many thanks to the Americans with Disabilities Act—she most definitely would have lost her job without it.

Home Again

The drive home was much like the weekend rides except for the dirty clothes and Zoe, the Great Dane, in the rear of the SUV. *Thank God we would never have to do this again.* We spoke amicably. Z told us about the new friends she had made and how she would hook up with them to attend the various meetings throughout our county as well as neighboring ones. We had become friendly with the parents of one of her new friends and they were nice, so my conclusion was that their daughter was nice, too.

I was correct in my assumption but still had a lot to learn about the disease and those that suffer from it. Z was our daughter, an honor student, beautiful, and a somewhat-talented chef. All she needed was love, support, and a nice place to live (that we would provide) until she got back on her feet. Oh boy, did I have a lot to learn. As I now look back, I'm sure that if you Google the word "codependency" my wife's and my face would show up on your computer screen.

I was glad to hear that Z was planning to attend either AA or NA meetings. The slogan for addicts newly released from treatment is "ninety meetings in ninety days." This is to encourage the newly out-of-treatment addict to stay on track. The feeling is that by attending ninety meetings one develops a daily routine that is a necessity, especially in early recovery. Complacency is one of the more significant causes of relapse. Getting into a routine can help to overcome the complacency that seems to develop after the addict is discharged from treatment. They often begin work, and suddenly the dream of "freedom" that they had (while in treatment) morphs into the reality of a life of hard work, meetings, and house chores. Developing a routine often removes the tediousness of forcing oneself to take each step of the day. Not having to think about what they have to do next just might allow them to drop the negative thoughts. Maybe they might begin to look at meetings, not just as a means to recovery, but also as a form of socialization.

I spoke to Z about outpatient therapy. She said that she was to start work in a week and that since she worked mornings she would try to attend the evening therapy sessions. This made me feel good. I had a feeling that this treatment was going to be the one and only. All the talk I had heard about the other girls relapsing and entering into one treatment after another *was not going to happen to my daughter.*

With me firmly pushing, we decided to continue attending the weekly Family Night meetings. I found them to be interesting as well as informative. I also felt that Z could use the input obtained there. These meetings not only help the addicts get through the hard times, but also teach the family about how to deal with an addict and to survive these hard times. Hopefully the treatment center where your loved one is attending offers this service.

We finally arrived home and Z and I unloaded her debris, bringing salvageable things into her room and those in need of decontamination to my wife, who manned the washing machine. It took several hours but at last there was a return, or rather an appearance of a return, to normalcy. At dinner we discussed the things that she would have to do during the following week: make preparations to attend her meetings and call her supervisor so that she could arrange to return to work. Keeping busy would help her focus on things other than her past addictions.

Something to keep in mind is that *you will be tempted to do a lot of the things that your loved one should be doing for themselves.* We, of course, began to do the research for her meetings, her laundry, and her cooking. This seemed natural to us as we had probably been doing it for most of the time she spent living with us. In hindsight, now we know that this is a habit we should have tried to beak as it could be a hindrance to recovery.

You will learn about codependency whether you educate yourself or not. To a certain extent we are all guilty of it. As you become more familiar with the term, you will likely find that you have been and will continue to be a codependent to your loved one. There are things that we do that we shouldn't that hinder our loved one's journey *toward independence*. Don't beat yourself up about it, but try to give your loved one enough space in their recovery to mature and learn to handle situations on their own. This will take some time and is one of the reasons they call this a "Family Disease." Washing Z's clothes, helping her find available meeting schedules, cooking for her, and preparing her to return to work were the very things that my daughter could and *should have* been doing on her own.

Dinner was enjoyable. We spoke a little about work and the meetings. She said that she was "meetinged out" and would like to take a day or two off before she began her ninety-meeting trek. I thought this sounded reasonable and agreed. She also said she would call her boss on Monday so that she could make arrangements to begin working as soon as possible. This too sounded great. I was feeling rather up at this point. I was confident that she would be all right. Every parent of an addict has this feeling right after a treatment ends, because every treatment leaves the addict with the potential to recover.

The next day Z announced that she had found an AA meeting to attend that night. She would be meeting some of the girls that she had befriended in treatment. Since we had been attending the Family Night meetings, we knew most of the girls and felt that this would be all right. Things were going as planned: she now had over thirty days clean and was on the right path, heading towards sixty. That would get her another chip.

Rehabilitation treatment is a necessity to *begin* the journey to sobriety, but the programs afterward are a necessity to *maintain* that sobriety. I was happy that she had found a meeting to go to and some friends that would be attending with her. Friends in sobriety are helpful support systems depending upon their time in recovery and their willingness to give support.

As good as I felt, there was always that little twang that stayed in a certain part of my brain and stomach that made me wonder if Z was really attending meetings when she said she was. This may be a horrible thing to think, but lying is a part of this disease and trust is something that is earned by loved ones over time—you may never be totally secure in their sobriety. Security and trust can only come with time, and you should never let an addict use them against you as a form of manipulation. For years, you may have been manipulated and lied to by someone who had developed an expertise in deceit so, and I know this may sound terrible, don't feel totally at fault for this lack of trust. Just know that if your loved one is truly working a program, you and their fellowship members will begin to develop a better sense of trust as time passes. The deceit and ability to lie so perfectly was not something that they developed to hurt their loved ones. It was *a survival mechanism* used to exist in the world of active addiction. Does this make their actions acceptable? Of course not! What it does is make them accountable for changing how they live—their concepts of right and wrong are not going to just change overnight like the snap of an on/off switch. Returning to the concept of sober existence is a change that they have to work on gradually, through working a program and therapy. First they have to see/admit that they were living a certain way to "survive"… and that it was going to destroy all their relationships and (very likely) eventually kill them.

So Z went to meetings and I, when not working, waited at home, hoping for her successful return (yep, codependency). To make the time pass, I did little things to keep busy but work was my greatest ally as well as an enemy. It took my thoughts off of the terrible possibilities that would creep into my mind when Z was out of sight, but it also kept me from observing her behavior. My wife, always the loving mother, didn't always pick up on the signs that Z was high. Many addicts enter into the pharmacy trying to fill prescriptions for intoxicants, so I do happen to be more cognizant of the signs. One of the hardest things to figure out is who legitimately needs these medications and who is trying to get their fix. One thing you learn fast in my chosen profession is that the addict is a smart and cunning deceiver. One of the hardest things for family members to do when their loved one is in recovery is to learn and accept that they have no control over when or if their loved one relapses.

You cannot prevent them from relapsing—this is one of the very few constants in this disease. Here are the three Cs of addiction recovery for family members: you didn't Cause it, you can't Cure it, and you can't Control it. You *might* become familiar enough with their behavior patterns to know when they are high. You *may even be able* to convince them to get help if you notice a problem arising. But you are *not the cause* of a relapse *nor can you be the savior* of your loved one if they do relapse. Yes, you may be able to force them to return to treatment but unless they are willing to actively participate in the treatment, your actions are useless.

Off Z went to her meetings, usually for an hour, and home she came. She mentioned that the girls had stopped to get coffee but that she hadn't since she had no money and was afraid that if she came home late, we would worry. I told her that a call would have alleviated the fear and that had she asked for a few dollars, I would have given it to her. I felt that the meetings should be enjoyable so that she would *want* to attend rather than feeling that she *had to*. I wanted to help as she had not started working yet. She had assured me she would begin work the next week.

I asked her if she had given any thought to getting a sponsor. She said she was looking for a sponsor that was a good fit with her personality. This too seemed logical. After all, this would be the go-to person that she would speak with when things seemed bad, as well as the one to guide her on her journey through the steps. It is a funny feeling for the parent to give up this piece of parenting. One must realize that there are certain things that we do not know and that only an addict can help another addict understand. Your family member has entered into a separate society. We may come close to understanding it, but we may never enter into it for we will never know the feelings involved with this disease unless we have had it. The hardest part of the treatment process is to give the addict the space that they need while watching as closely as possible. Keep in mind that it is not an easy task, to be the parent or loved one of an addict. You may have to suddenly give up what you feel are your parental or family rights to protect your loved one. This is part of *setting boundaries* as well as allowing your loved one the space to mature emotionally.

My daughter was like a whole new person. An addict once said to me that when your family member is straight, you don't have to ask if they are straight. This is so true. I had lived with a stoned daughter for so long that I had forgotten what she was like straight. Her state of high became the norm and the family became accustomed to this. But as she never came home overtly high, falling all over herself, it was difficult to notice that she had changed. I can only assume that she allowed herself to "come down" enough so that she was able to function before returning home. I could now see the difference and it was wonderful.

She was no longer "so tired" that she would fall asleep while we were talking. She no longer had to "get things at the store" at midnight only to return home two hours later, rushing to her room, locking her door, and not emerging until early the next afternoon. Despite this, she always had a good work ethic. High or straight, she went to work. As I think back, I wonder how she functioned as well as she did under the circumstances.

Now, she woke early, spoke clearly, and was alert. She continued to attend meetings although she began to favor NA over AA. She came home from a meeting that first week having found a sponsor. One of the most important events in an addict's journey towards long-term sobriety is finding a sponsor, so that was wonderful news. A good sponsor can help an addict avoid relapse by helping them understand how to get through the Twelve Steps of the program. The Twelve Steps are what teach the addict how to understand what living life is about. It helps them to organize their perception of how to get through life in a functional manner.

As a matter of fact, the book *Alcoholics Anonymous* by Bill Wilson, often referred to as the Big Book, and the Twelve Steps are something that us "normies" (an affectionate term for those not in the program) should also read and try to live by. It is a great reference text for good living. It is also the basis for the family-oriented programs such as Al-Anon and Nar-Anon.

My daughter's life was now consumed with work and meetings. She found a home group that she liked in a nearby town and seemed to attend most of her meetings there. She often spoke about a guy who chaired many of the meetings whom she respected for his knowledge and insight into this disease. I was truly impressed. Deep down, I had a hunch he was also attractive to her but I said nothing of this since, for the first year, romance is discouraged. The saying that a therapist friend of mine teaches is "Don't date 'til you're an eight." This means that dating should be postponed until your self-esteem has risen to the level of eight out of ten. When asked how they would know when this level had been attained, she would reply, "When you don't have to ask."

My wife and daughter continued to join me at Family Night. Family and alumni are encouraged to attend these meetings. Alumni are those who have completed the course of therapy. This is important, since once they've left the rehab center, the addict develops different emotional experiences that they are not sure how to handle. For likely a long period of time they have been living in a world of irrational behavior, not having the ability to process their actions (drugs had numbed many of their experiences). Now, "back in society" as a sober person they may be totally confused as to how to act. Most clients don't have insurance and cannot afford to pay for therapy, so both the Family Night therapist and various alumni can be a great help in reassuring the addict at this time.

Insecurities and anxieties are normal and to be told this from an addiction professional and from those who have been through it all is of great positive consequence. It is these negative feelings that, *if left to grow and fester*, can lead to relapse. The process of relapse starts long before the actual relapse occurs—hopefully it can be caught and halted before it progresses to the end stage.

Therefore, every Tuesday we would get into the car and attend the meeting together. I would devour all the information put forth and when alone I would try to analyze it. I was determined to learn as much as possible about this red-headed step-child of disease states. I also noticed a bond forming between us and the other parents who chose to attend on a weekly basis. Little by little, we became quasi families.

Sadly, many clients were young and from out of state. They had no families to attend the meeting and felt scared, depressed, and alone. When called upon to discuss what was bothering them they would often mention how envious they were of those who had family who could attend meetings. We would often act as surrogate family members, offering advice that, for the time being, was eagerly accepted.

That addicts are criminals who have no souls and don't care about what they do or how they act couldn't be farther from the truth. In my journey through the recovery process with Z, I've met addicts with college degrees and addicts who could not read. Sober addicts who regularly attend meetings have something in common: they care and will try to help those who are trying to recover. To not have had the opportunity to make their acquaintance would be a missed learning experience. They can positively affect and change your concept of this disease and all those who suffer from it.

Relapse

Things went well for about three months. I was happy as she would come home from the meetings and show me and her mom the key chains that she received as she attended Narcotics Anonymous meetings. It seems as if each key tag brought renewed sense of pride as she attached the various-colored tags to each other. Then I started to notice some changes in Z. At first they were subtle. She would come home from work a little later than usual, she would come home from a meeting past midnight, and worst of all, she would sometimes fall asleep on the couch. She claimed she was still attending meetings and Family Night and always had a semi-acceptable excuse for her lateness or sleepiness. It was due to how "hard she worked." (And chefs do work hard.) It was that she had to "be at work at six in the morning and attend a late-night meeting and then see her friends for coffee."

I had a growing sickening feeling that relapse was a possibility, but Z and my wife assured me I was wrong. So I settled into parental paranoia. This lack of trust on the parental end is also part of the disease.

I think it was about the beginning of the fourth month of sobriety that someone at Family Night mentioned that Z didn't look all that well. She was confronted and submitted to a drug test (which she passed) but then refused to return to further meetings, as did my wife. That was the end of Family Nights for Z. She claimed she was mad because they had no right to test her and cause her embarrassment as she was no longer a client there and my wife was just happy to not have to worry about being asked any questions by the therapist. I, though upset with them, wanted to continue to learn and perhaps provide some solid parental support to the clients, so I continued to attend. Z's decline was slow and steady—or so I thought.

She claimed to still be attending NA meetings. I hoped with all my heart that she was being truthful, but unfortunately, lying is an integral part of this disease and unless I attended with her there was no way that I could actually know for sure, and this is something that I could not and should not do—at that point I would not have bet the family farm on it. I could only encourage Z to attend them. She was the addict; she needed to make the decision to attend. Sorry for the redundancy here, but you cannot *cause someone suffering from this disease to use nor can you be their savior*. I will mention this many more times and hopefully you will believe me eventually, but don't beat yourself up if you don't: you wouldn't be alone. If she did use, I could only hope that it was a slip and not a relapse. Neither is good but a slip is something that is very short term and usually a spur of the moment thing. The addict picks up, without planning to do so, and realizes they did wrong and immediately goes back to their recovery. A relapse on the other hand is usually a planned event and if there is a return to sobriety it occurs over a longer period of time. Death can occur in either case.

The important thing to ask is: if she had relapsed (deep down inside I knew that she had but tried hard to believe that this had not occurred—once again *denial* rears its ugly head), what could I have done to change this? Perhaps I could have persuaded her to return to treatment. Could she have returned without my push to? Of course she could have, but *she didn't want to*. Maybe she was suffering from shame due to the relapse. There could have been many reasons why she did not ask for help or that I didn't intervene. The fact is she didn't, and most likely my intervention would have been met with resistance from both my daughter and my wife. In all honesty, to some extent both my wife and I were guilty of not speaking to Z enough and certainly Z was guilty of not admitting to her relapse. The fault lies on my daughter as she is the only one who can admit to her problem and ask for help. The truth is, once an addict relapses, even before they start to use drugs again, little can be done to stop the progression of the relapse. As previously stated, a relapse is something that occurs over time. It may start with thought of using and finally progress to the point where the patient finally uses the drug. A relapse is not a spur of the moment happening. It involves a progressive evolution from behavioral changes to the actual act of using. It is the one who suffers from the disease who must make the decision to seek help.

One night as the phone rang at 1 am all I could think was that either Z had been arrested, had an accident, or worse, had overdosed. I was right on worry #2: it was Z calling to say she had been driving home from a meeting, a cat ran out in front of the car (my wife's), she went up on the center medium of the street, and now could not drive the car home. She was waiting for a tow truck and asked if I could pick her up as the police wouldn't drive her home.

Up I got, dressed, and off I went to pick her up. Before I left, I asked my wife if perhaps now she believed that Z was getting high. My wife, ever the mother, exclaimed that perhaps an animal did run in front of the car. She then pointed out that I myself was guilty of swerving to avoid hitting an animal on several occasions.

So I bit my tongue and drove to the scene of the accident. A policeman sat in his car, filling out the usual paperwork. I introduced myself to him. He didn't seem to know what had happened, so I thanked him and proceeded to the car. There was my daughter, asleep in the front seat; I opened the door, tapped her, and she woke. When I asked what had happened, she repeated the cat story. I slowly walked around the car to see what damage had been done. The front fender was dented. I could only assume that had happened when she jumped the curb. There were clumps of grass stuck in the wheels but all in all, the damage didn't seem excessive. I asked why she was on this particular street as it was not on the direct route (from where she had said the NA meeting was) to our home. "I was looking for a short cut," was her response. I asked how she was able to fall asleep so quickly after the accident. She told me to lower my voice so the policeman would not hear. Why did I have to speak quietly? She said she had had to get to work extra early that day and was tired.

How to figure out if she was truly straight? I waited with her until the tow truck arrived and then had to wake her again. The drive home was silent. She went to bed immediately. The next few days consisted of me trying to convince my wife that we once again had a problem and speaking numerous times with the insurance company. They finally declared the car a total loss and cut us a check. I asked the insurance adjuster why he was totaling the car out as I had seen only minimal damage. His response was courteous but to the point. He said that the car had hit the median at a high rate of speed. The entire undercarriage of the car had been torn to pieces. She was traveling at a high rate of speed and fell asleep or something else had caused her to leave the road and drive up on the median. Perhaps this information would be enough to convince my wife.

That weekend we bought a nice Kia Soul that came with all kinds of warranties and looked cute. My wife was happy. Z could only use the car to go to and from work but she eventually convinced my wife to allow her to use the car to go to meetings. I objected, but busy with work, I finally caved under the pressure, feeling as any parental enabler would that if she attended meetings, then perhaps she would again recover before things got too far out of hand. This of course never happened. Probably she wasn't attending any meetings, either.

What did happen was several months later she got into another accident. I figured that perhaps I better pay for this myself so that the insurance company would not drop me. Clever person that I am, it cost me $5000 and then the insurance company dropped me anyway for *totaling the previous car*. What I should have done was *make her take the bus to work instead of enabling her*. That would have ensured other drivers on the road weren't endangered.

We drove the car to the body shop and there was my upset wife, my upset me, and my sleeping daughter. I motioned towards Z and my wife was not sure what to make of what she was seeing. "Do you think she got a concussion in the accident?" I answered no, but that I would love to give her one. We got a rental car to add to the expense so that my daughter could get to work (enabling, I know). We drove home and Z slept until it was time to go to work.

It is truly amazing the length that a family can extend itself in order to rationalize enabling. My wife and I did it very well. A therapist at one of the meetings I attend likes to illustrate the following about the word rationalize: break the word into two, change the z to an s, and you get *ration lies*. Oh how easy it is to allow yourself to continue to ration those lies your loved one tells you while maintaining a guiltless perspective of your own actions.

At the Family Night meeting after the second accident, the therapist explained to me why what I was doing was considered *enablement*. I was somewhat embarrassed but totally aware that what I did was wrong. I never should have allowed Z to use the car again. There are plenty of people who take public transportation to get to work. She should have been left on her own to find a way to get to work and anywhere else she was going. This is what therapists refer to as *setting boundaries*. Instead, we continued to provide for her, making it easier for her, not just to go to work, but to continue to travel down her path towards destruction.

As time passed, I began to realize just how wrong my actions were. I guess life is funny. On the one hand, had Z entered into long-term recovery (fighting each day to remain sober), this would not have been considered enabling; but as she was in active addiction or relapsing, it was wrong and it is only hindsight that will help you understand the concept of enabling. It can be difficult to grasp that you are enabling someone at the time that you are doing it. Let us suppose that you have a child who goes to school, works hard and wants to open a business. He is short of funds to do so, so he applies for a loan. He is told that he needs a cosigner to get the loan so he asks you. You know that he is responsible, hard-working, and an entrepreneur. The possibility of the business becoming successful outweighs the chances of failure because of your child's work ethic and his knowledge of the business. So you therefore cosign for your child. This is helping your child get a start in life. Now, let us assume your child has just come out of treatment a month ago. He is living with you, goes to meetings but comes home late, stays in his room, refuses to speak to you about his sobriety and then asks you to co-sign for a small business loan. You think that this will help him gain some responsibility and stay straight. In this situation, you don't even know if he is sober, he is just out of treatment and his actions show a possibility of a potential relapse. Cosigning in this case would be considered enabling.

One Family Night, a young lady had completed her in-house treatment and had made arrangements to enter into a sober living facility. Her parents had come to visit and to assist her in the move. They had paid for the first two weeks rent so she would have time to find a job, accumulate money to buy food and other necessities, and get back on her feet. So far so good. Towards the end of the meeting, the client announced that she had decided to return home with her parents rather than enter into sober living. The mother told her she should go to sober living and couldn't return home. The father, however, told her that she had been away from home long enough and could come home. He would support her until she found a job and felt that she was under enough pressure having this disease and didn't need any more brought on by having to support herself. The therapist brought it up for discussion. No one agreed with the father. He took this as a personal attack and brought the daughter home. This is an example of enabling. A very dangerous example that could possibly lead to a relapse.

The trouble with this disease is that you don't always get the time to make corrections as you never know when your loved one's using might be their last. Yes, this does sound very melodramatic but as you become more familiar with this disease you will also become more familiar with how deadly it is. You should also be aware that although I make a point of how dangerous enabling is, I also realize *how hard it is to stop doing it*. This is especially true for parents who haven't reached the point of *compassion fatigue*. I know a therapist who tells the Family Night group about how her child was addicted to heroin and she was addicted to helping her child. You will be told that enabling is dangerous and could be deadly—this is true. It is also easier to *say* you are going to stop doing it than to *actually stop* doing it.

Meanwhile, the pill mill situation was getting totally out of hand. Something would have to be done. Until reelections are jeopardized, not much often occurs in situations like this. Then suddenly all hell breaks loose and heads begin to roll. Remember those pharmacists I mentioned? The ones that called the DEA to ask if it was legal to fill those prescriptions and were told yes? Well, when the end is near, those words are forgotten and suddenly those pharmacists are being arrested. Is the DEA wrong? Yes and no! Any licensed professional should know what is going on. If you fill opiate prescriptions to make money, knowing that they are probably going to be used for illegal purposes, you are a pusher like any other drug pusher. Most pharmacists keep these ambiguous prescriptions to a minimum. There are some pharmacists who just don't care who they hurt. They forget that those children walking in from the pill mills are someone's child…that somewhere there is a heartbroken family member trying to survive this tragedy…that they are turning a healthy person into someone who will suffer from a lifelong disease from which there is no cure. The rationale for the pharmacist may be, "if I don't fill the prescriptions, it's not as if that is the end of the story. The person will find a pharmacy that will, so why should I be the one to pass up a high-profit opportunity? On the other hand, the DEA's response should have been, "As a professional, you must decide if the prescription is used for legitimate purposes." If the pharmacist sees an excess of opiate prescriptions for young patients who appear high and not in medical need of these prescriptions, he/she has a professional responsibility to *not fill* them.

    The pharmacies and doctors make lots of money—the driving force behind any business. Insurance companies and major chains that make unbelievable profits have driven the independent pharmacists and doctors out of business with no conscience at all. There is a lot of blame to spread around. The independent pharmacist goes to jail for twenty years and the chain pharmacies pay a multimillion-dollar slap-on-the-wrist fine. The independent's life is rightfully ruined but the chain *isn't even affected* by the fine. For the family and the addict, there is only devastation, no matter from whom or where they get their drugs, for they are left with a disease with a better-than-average chance of ending in death.

    For the new family involved in the recovery process, relapses are often hard to spot. Initially the addict, a master of deception, can keep their drug-induced stupor hidden. Z was no exception.

Relapse often takes the addict right back to where they had left off before they last entered treatment. What this means is that when an addict relapses they don't "start out" as they did when they first started using drugs—on a recreational basis—but rather, upon relapse, they use as one who is already addicted to drugs. The detection problem lies with the fact that they now know that *you know* that they have a drug problem, so they go to greater lengths to hide their intoxication. Under the "cover" of attending NA meetings, Z would come home late. I can only assume that she was waiting until she could maintain an appearance of sobriety before coming home thus avoiding having a confrontation with my wife or me. She would leave the house to buy something "at the store" only to return hours later. As previously stated, this went on for several months. But the body can only take so much abuse before the signs become more obvious.

One day you might enter their room and find them sleeping half on the bed and half on the floor or…perhaps they passed out in the bathroom. Hopefully a tap or a shove will wake them. Z would awaken startled, and the lies would begin to flow. She was "cleaning her closet" and was tired so she laid her head upon the bed for a second and "must have fallen asleep." She simply must take some time off from work as she "is much too tired." As the disease progresses, the lies become less believable but for some reason we accept what they say and are thankful for the few moments of peace. Whether it be that we wanted to avoid conflict, or that damn enabling factor arose, or maybe we were just plain tired of the conflict. Maybe it was simply that we are so absolutely thankful that they *woke up* when we tapped them, and we keep hoping that somehow a miracle will occur and they will be back in recovery. The addicted member is not the only one to think in an irrational manner. As that smart therapist said: your loved one is addicted to their drug of choice and you are addicted to them.

Z would come home from work daily, greet whomever happened to be around, and lock herself in her room. The lock on her door was bothersome to me. She was entitled to some privacy but I was uncomfortable with the idea that in an emergency it would be difficult to get into her room. I had mentioned this on several occasions but never pushed forward with a lock removal plan. It was one of those things that we put on our to-do list. Were we trying to avoid a conflict, or perhaps just guilty of seeking an advanced degree in procrastination? Well, like so many things that we never get around to doing, this eventually came back to bite us on the ass.

One day Z returned from work a little later than usual. She walked by me and into her room without the usual greeting and shut the door. A few minutes later my wife came into the room and asked if Z was home and I said yes, that something must be up because she zipped right into her room and didn't stop to speak to anyone.

My wife had been waiting for her as she wanted to ask her something, so she knocked on her door—no answer. She then banged on the door—still no answer. She tried to open it—locked. She called me in a panicky voice. I was on the verge of napping on the living room couch and it took a few moments for me to gather my thoughts and stand up.

"What's wrong?" I asked.

"She's not answering her door!" At that point I pounded on the door—no answer. Finally my wife found the spare key and unlocked it. There was Z on the bed, in what appeared to be a coma, with a blue tint on her face. My wife started screaming and crying, and I quickly felt for a pulse and shouted to our other daughter to call 911 when I didn't feel one.

I then began CPR. Thank God for the CPR training that I had taken to be qualified to administer vaccines. I continued to give CPR as my other daughter spoke with the emergency dispatcher, which can be frustrating. (Even though you know rationally they have to ask the questions.) After what seemed like an eternity, I heard the sirens and knew that help was on the way. The time lapse was only a matter of minutes as the fire station is only about two miles away, but to a parent working on a seemingly dead family member and worrying about brain damage and any other side effects that comes with anoxia, time has no reality. The dispatcher told my daughter that the ambulance had arrived and that she should allow them to come directly into the house.

They immediately took over the rescue effort. While one paramedic placed an oxygen mask over her face, two others put her on the stretcher, started an IV, and administered a dose of Narcan. Narcan is a drug that almost immediately counteracts the action of an opiate. Within seconds, Z jumped up, asking what was going on. By this time the police had arrived and were asking questions. I looked at her bed and saw a syringe and spoon. I felt nauseous and had to suppress the urge to throw up.

When I worked as a hospital pharmacist I had seen overdoses in the emergency room and had been able to maintain my professionalism. This however, was my daughter—my reaction was different. The policeman could tell the extent of our distress. He put the bedcover over her paraphernalia and looked me in the eye and asked if she had ever had a seizure before. My first reaction was surprise then I regained my composure and said no, this was a first. He finalized his report that stated that she had possibly suffered a seizure. I thanked him as the paramedics placed her into the ambulance that we followed to the hospital.

When we arrived, she was sitting up and speaking to the nurse, who shot us a look of sympathy. Z was now feeling nauseous so the nurse brought her an emesis basin and told her to try to aim straight. She puked a few times and felt a little better. My wife suggested that perhaps she was nauseous from the fright that she had just experienced. I knew better though. Most addicts get nauseous form the opiate and believe it or not they seem to accept this as part of the high and often enjoy this feeling. At this time my daughter, due to the Narcan, was no longer high and most definitely not enjoying it. There should be consequences for what had just happened so we let her enjoy the puking and the withdrawal that came with the use of Narcan. It was the poor aide that had to clean up after her (the emesis basin doth runneth over) that I had the compassion for.

While sitting there, I suggested that she call her boss to tell him that she would not be at work the next day. She agreed, claiming that perhaps a day to rest up after almost dying was just what she needed. I then told her that was just what she didn't need. What she needed was a second trip to the Detox center and then to Rehab. She protested, claiming that she could get clean by attending meetings. I knew that this was bull as at this point in time she had no thoughts of getting straight or entering into recovery and she had a hunch that I knew this as I handed the phone to her and told her to call. This accomplished, I then had her call Rehab. The process was set in motion. We were to bring her to the Detox center at 10 am the next day and the treatment process was to begin again.

AA and NA meetings work for those who have their mind set on getting straight and have been through Detox—a very dangerous process that requires trained medical supervision. If the addict is hell-bent on recovering and has a support group who will work with them, the meetings will work. For most addicts, getting and staying straight requires more than meetings. My daughter is a perfect example. I was thankful to the treatment center for having the Family Night meetings. They taught me a lot about the disease and the difference in my knowledge and my wife's, who had decided to not attend these meetings, was significant. I cannot stress enough the advantage knowledge can provide you in dealing with this disease.

One can see the difference in the actions of family members who attend the Family Night meetings versus those who do not. This is because there, they have the opportunity to learn to understand when their loved one is trying to manipulate them. For instance, Z definitely tried to stop me from trying to push her into treatment. I might have believed her when she said she could get straight on her own had I not been to Family Nights and heard all the stories. I could clearly see that she had no intention of doing so and just wanted to get home to procure some heroin to escape the withdrawal she was now going through.

We are often told that if the addict is forced into treatment it will not work, but I was willing to take this chance with Z as, yes, *sometimes it can*. Yes, you can and should exert some pressure on your loved one to enter into a rehab program but keep in mind that successful treatment is dependent upon the determination of the addict to participate in the healing. Although there is a more positive outlook for the addict that chooses to enter into treatment on their own, even that is no guarantee of success.

Now we're back to: if your loved one relapsed it was *not due to anything that you did or for a lack of their love* for you. If love was enough to keep the addicted member from relapsing there would be a lot fewer relapses. Just as for the first-time addict, treatment for relapse is a two-phase process. The first phase is the physical process: Detox. They detoxify for whatever time is needed (or that they can afford, or that insurance will pay for) to get them off the drug or drugs that they are using. They are treated with medication on a tapering basis; upon completion the medication will be discontinued. The second phase, Rehab, is psychological. This is a subjective process where the therapists try to work their magic to uncover what it was that drew your loved one to the usage of their substances of choice and why they cannot seem to stop using them. The success of the second phase, the psychological one, is dependent on the attitude and outlook of the patient. This is why your support is often a necessary factor as the patient suffering from the disease of addiction suffers also from low self-esteem (and guilt for the physical and emotional distress that this disease has caused their family).

So Z went back, giving my wife and me another five-week grace period in which we hoped she was safe and doing well and didn't suddenly decide to leave. That weekend when we visited her at the Detox center she seemed a little shaky. This we now knew was to be expected. We hugged and sat down at a table and let her direct the conversation. At this point of withdrawal the addict is usually not feeling up to snuff and should not be given any more stress than what they are already handling. This is a terrible time for them. If you attend meetings such as NA or AA, you will often hear the addicts share that it is much easier to *stay* straight than to *get* straight. This, however, is something that someone suffering from the disease of addiction seems to have no trouble setting aside when they are ready to relapse.

The facility my daughter attended had a gourmet chef. For many clients, this facility was the first "normal living" they'd had in several years with clean rooms, good food, and tender treatment. Unfortunately, most are too ill to actually take advantage of the facility. Quite often when they are released to the Rehab center they feel worse than when they were in Detox.

So we allowed Z to direct the conversation. She told us that she had scored some black tar heroin on the way home from work. She was feeling sick since work was busy, and she had been feeling particularly uneasy. She went directly to her room that night, locked the door, and the last thing that she remembered before waking to a room full of police and paramedics was cooking the heroin and drawing it up into the syringe. She didn't remember the injection process at all. She saw no lights at the end of a tunnel. There was nothing, just waking up to a commotion and finding out that she had experienced her first overdose. All I could think to say was, "Hopefully this will be the last."

I had heard too many stories of beautiful, intelligent people who had overdosed many times and still relapsed or worse, didn't make it. If my wife hadn't tried to enter Z's room to ask a question that horrible night, we might have been in mourning instead. I now (finally) realized that my daughter was no exception: she was an addict. Intelligence, good looks, a good background—none of these factor into the world of addiction. Well, other than the fact that if you continue to use, you will lose your perspective concerning all of these factors.

My protective shield of denial that Z's outcome would differ from others had been shattered. We stayed for our allotted time and then left. When the reality surfaces and the addiction is again acted upon, depression is the most common reaction. We were no exception. We went out to dinner that evening and after returning home I called a close friend who is like family who had spent some time in recovery. He was both comforting and knowledgeable and I asked if he would attend an Al-Anon meeting with me. He agreed.

Later that week I attended two meetings. I went to Family Night and the therapist spoke with me and opened it up to the floor for input. I found this comforting and therapeutic. Until one gets the opportunity to release stored-up tensions in a therapeutic setting, the importance of doing so cannot be appreciated. So don't listen to friends and family who may refer to therapy as bull.

It's you who are suffering and not them. It is easy to give advice to someone when you haven't experienced what they are going through. Later in the week my friend and I attended an Al-Anon meeting. (These are very similar to AA and NA meetings and will be discussed later.) They can and often do save your emotional life and marriage. So, yes you come home from work tired, resent your addict family member for the life they have imposed upon you, and now you have to attend another meeting. Don't sweat the little things. Attend these meetings. They are extremely therapeutic. After living with an addict for a period of time, we do learn how to live a normal life again. An added advantage of these meetings is that you meet people who are in the same situation as you are and that you can relate to. You often form bonds and friendships that last forever.

But most important you, like the addict, have a support group to go to when things get tough. We normies, like the addict, often think that what we are going through is unique to us. We tend to hold these feelings of shame and guilt in for whatever reason, and allow them to fester. By attending these meetings and listening to others' stories, you will find that your situation is more common than you thought. This is what makes going to meetings so valuable. So try to attend at least one meeting per week. Never forget that this is a family disease. It does not affect just the person suffering from the disease of addiction; it also affects the family members (sometimes worse than it does the addict).

The following week I attended Family Night and spoke with the therapist and some of the other family members who I had bonded with over the past year. They expressed their sorrow about Z's relapse and extended hope for the best. My story was not at all uncommon and in the past I too had hugged other family members and expressed my support to them. I had also experienced a family's loss of an addicted family member. The sorrow that you feel cannot easily be expressed. It is more than mourning the death of a friend's family member for this is something that you now realize you too could be going through at any moment while your family member is using. You also can't help but feel how unnecessary the death was since this is a disease of choice.

RELAPSE

Yes, it is a choice, *up until the addiction overtakes your loved one's thinking* process. Prior to that point they can enter into treatment, attend sessions with a therapist, and enter into a program that they must work with a passion to maintain their sobriety. Since I am not one who suffers from this disease I cannot describe the urges or sensations that are involved when a relapse occurs. The only thing that I can say to a mother or father reading this is that the bond associated with parenthood can only be felt by a parent. The strength of this bond can make a mother or father forfeit their life so that their child may live.

Yet, on many occasions I have witnessed situations where a parent risked the loss of a child in order to satisfy their urge to use drugs. For example, a parent who is on probation and has just gotten custody of their child back from Child Protective Services, comes to a meeting. They have been clean and sober for six months and express how wonderful it is to be able to have their children back, and to once again be living at home. There are hugs and tears as the fellowship creates bonds among the members. This continues hopefully forever. Importunely this is not always the case. Sometimes, and this is not all that unusual, you begin to see a change in the behavior pattern. A sadness seems to creep in or they just act different. It is not always easy to pinpoint but you can sense that something is not right.

This may continue or it may disappear. Hopefully the latter. Recovery is never a smooth trip; it has its ups and downs as life does. Hence the need for meetings, therapy, support groups, and the working of the program on a continuing basis. Sometimes, however, the person loses control and the bad feelings lead to a relapse and the state once again steps in and takes the children. It is then that the state must make a decision as to whether the children are put in temporary custody or if the decision will be permanent. This is a terrible time, for the addict is aware of what is happening but they have no control over their use. Yes, some may go into treatment but some can't seem to be able to make that decision. I can't tell you why and neither can a therapist but this most powerful bond, that of a mother and child, is not strong enough to overcome the urges associated addiction. This urge to use goes against the laws of nature. When clean and in treatment these same parents cry and beg for the return of their children yet when in active addiction and craving a fix they cannot control their thinking. This is a concept that someone who has not lived through it can never believe or understand. I have personally witnessed this. You just sit there and listen and on the inside your heart tears in two, and you want to grab them and shake them and scream, but you watch, knowing that they have passed the point that words, at least for a while, will not help. This is only one of the reasons that I tell loved ones not to try to understand this disease: even the addict cannot figure out why they do what they do. This may sound a bit confusing as I keep saying that you should try to learn as much about this disease as possible and now I am saying do not try to understand. What I mean is that while the addict is in active addiction, *they cannot be understood.* As you gain knowledge, I feel that you will hopefully develop ways to deal with the disease and your loved one but always remember: when using, your loved one does not know why they do what they do. We/they may be able to rationalize what they do but we may never understand *why* they do it.

    I was sitting in a chair, thinking about all the meetings and advice that I have given over time. Some of the advice was good and some, the therapist had to correct me on. I can only guess that this is part of the learning process. I was still in deep thought, waiting for the meeting to begin, when suddenly the clients began to enter the room. The Druggy Buggy, as the van that transports the clients to meetings is affectionately called, had arrived and so had my daughter. She sat in a chair next to me and the therapist called the meeting to order. We introduced ourselves and spoke about why we were there. I had been attending the meetings by myself for so long that I now felt strange with my daughter sitting next to me. I wished my wife would have also attended but she was afraid of having to speak at the meeting and I could only guess that there was a certain amount of shame involved too. I could understand her feelings but I also could not help but think about how much Z needed her support. I remembered hearing clients say how much they wished that their parents could attend the meetings. I was there, and I would offer all the support that I could and at home her mother would do the same. My wife's feelings about attending the meetings are by no means unique. Quite often a family member will refuse to attend, often without reason. All I can offer is that if they absolutely refuse to attend it is probably better for the addicted member of the family if they stay at home if it is likely they may act abusively.

To my surprise, the therapist did not speak with my daughter that evening. I made a mental note to ask the therapist why before the next meeting started. I listened to the other clients and their families and offered advice from a parent's—with almost sixty years of living experience—point of view. Sometimes life allows a view from a different perspective so that we can learn. For this reason, the therapist always opens the discussion up to the families for input. I do suggest, however, that you have reached a point of composure first, thus allowing for a more rational thought process. The clients can have, especially when they are just coming into treatment from the Detox center, pent-up repressed anger if they are not fully detoxed. Their comments are sometimes found by their loved ones to be antagonistic. Like a caterpillar metamorphosizing into a beautiful butterfly, so too will you see your loved one change from an often-nasty, mean-spirited person to a friendly, loving person. This will take place and you will see the change weekly if you attend the meetings.

Later that week, I attended another Al-Anon meeting with my friend and noticed that I was starting to learn from a different point of view. At Family Night we learned how to help the addict succeed with their treatment and about how *not* to enable our loved ones (enabling hinders their attempt at recovery). At Al-Anon though, we were learning how to *succeed in living our own lives* as well as how to survive this sinister disease. These do not always run parallel but continued attendance can start to change that.

I was sure that my daughter would lose her job due to this relapse. She had notified her superiors that she was hospitalized and would be out of work for about five weeks. They were not thrilled with the prospect of covering her shifts but the Americans with Disabilities Act protected her. They called the house a few times, asking when she would return and if she was doing okay, but confidentiality prevented them from asking what was wrong and we were not offering any information so they could only guess—you cannot fire someone on a guess. For the time being she was safe and her health coverage was still in effect. I'm sure due to such a high rate of addiction in Z's field that they had a strong suspicion as to what she was being "hospitalized" for.

The following week I arrived early to ask the therapist why she had not spoken with my daughter at the last meeting. She explained that she found that during the first week in Rehab after coming from Detox, the client is usually still going though withdrawal and their responses are not yet totally legitimate. She had therefore learned to wait until the second Family Night after Rehab admission to begin the discussion process. She said that she had, however, worked with her in the group session. The group sessions were held the following morning and the therapist would work on things brought up at Family Night or that the therapist might have entered into the patients' notes.

"I worked with her both from what the therapist at Detox had noted and from what I had gathered from your input over time when you would speak about Z." I responded that I had complete confidence in her ability and that my question was in no way to be construed as criticism. I agreed that many of the clients did seem to still be withdrawing the first week of Family Night, although I thought that as society begins to accept this as a disease, perhaps the treatment will progress and allow for a longer stay in Detox so that this would someday no longer be a problem. She agreed and thanked me for my input, saying that if there was an upside to this epidemic it was that as family members learn about it, they are more likely to accept addiction as a disease.

And so, after the Druggy Buggy arrived again, week two began. The therapist spoke to another family before she turned her attention to my daughter and me. No matter how many meetings you attend, when another client and family is being interacted with it is different than when it is you. The fact is that it's nerve-wracking to be interviewed in front of others.

First, their eyes are on you but nothing is said. They appear to be in deep thought, trying to formulate a way to pierce that armor that has shielded you from the reality of your life for so long that you no longer believe that there is a problem. Yet, you have a family member who is an addict, and this therapist has spoken with them, and whether you or they are right, a problem exists. (Otherwise you wouldn't be sitting there, wondering if anyone would notice if you crawled under your chair.) What I had going for me was that this was time number two and she *didn't have to convince me* that my daughter was an addict or that she did indeed belong in a facility. What Z had going for her was that this was her second treatment and she knew that she had really screwed up this time (having been only seconds away from death). What the therapist had going for her was that she could start working on our problems right away. What a sad win-win-win situation. Nevertheless, what she said seemed like common sense until I realized that I *never would have thought of this or that* much less connected it to this disease.

She was tough but kind, giving sympathy when necessary but not allowing us to pull one single fiber of wool over her eyes. Clients clearly resent this at first but once they have finally attainted a state of sobriety they at the very least have respect for her (or him). I never heard a negative comment about her from a client who was serious about their recovery.

Next, it was my time on the firing block. There were the piercing eyes, the silence, and the urge to have a reason to use the men's room so that I could escape. I was glad that it was my turn, but discussing family problems in front of the group was challenging to say the least. I made a great effort to be truthful without creating friction within the family. I found that when cornered, my daughter would bring up any negativities that may have been mentioned concerning another family member, trying to manipulate the situation in her favor. For example, if I had ever said to Z, "I think that Mom should be at the Family Night meetings," later, when cornered, she would blame her relapse on the fact that Mom didn't attend the meetings and that even Dad had said so. Don't be surprised if your loved tries to throw you under the bus—they will. It is a tactic used to avert your attention from their relapse. You shouldn't take anything they say to heart as they will lash out to cover the fact that they are either using, or are about to. They'll seek revenge for the fact that you are aware of the situation. Try to keep in mind that *this is the disease speaking*. Yes, it is your loved one making the vitriolic performance, but if not in a relapse mode post Detox, they probably would never act that way.

I decided that this was a situation that I could live with since my daughter's well being was more important than other family members hearing of a seemingly negative comment that I may make. The words began to flow. I spoke of my wife's denial of the situation until it had come to a head and exploded. I spoke of how Z seemed to love the life of the addict and until this could be remedied, I saw little hope for extended sobriety. My daughter disagreed with me, saying that almost dying gave her a new perspective on life and she was serious about renewing her sobriety.

All you can do is give support and hope that the truth is being spoken. The trouble is that *trust must be earned*. So although you can always hope for the best, there is always that sickening feeling that remains that hopefully fades as sober time progresses. It's "sickening" in its true sense: you may feel a little ill knowing that you are being played or that your loved one is truly not into working towards a recovery. Until you get to the point when you really believe that you are *not responsible* for your loved one using, you have the potential to *carry the guilt of their addiction*.

In this disease, no one is totally free from fault although the only one responsible for the use of drugs is the one who uses. The bottom line is that the addict is the one who makes the decision to use and the blame rests with them. I've often heard it said that the addict starts using recreationally, never expecting to become an addict. They do start recreationally, but they also do know that the drugs that they use, the Oxys and Benzos, have the potential for addiction and like playing Russian roulette with a loaded gun, eventually you will become an addict, just like the gun will kill you if you pull the trigger enough times.

The weeks passed and soon it was almost time for her to be released. The head therapist called, asking us to come in for our family interview. This is frequently done for those family members who live locally or are able to travel to the center before the release date of the client. If you don't live in the area (frequently the case), this meeting will most likely occur via the telephone or perhaps online. Since we would meet with her therapist in an office, alone, my wife felt this was both important and safe.

We sat in the lobby, waiting to meet with the therapist, tensions high. I had never been through this before and didn't know what to expect, as there hadn't been an exit interview last time. We sat and waited and read the addiction paraphernalia on the table. Finally, out came the therapist. She brought us into her office and sent for Z.

We exchanged greetings and she got down to the purpose of the meeting. She told us that although our daughter's outlook was considerably better this time around, she still needed more structured support. She suggested a halfway house or perhaps a month-long stay at their after-care facility, referred to as "transient living." She told us that the transient living facility was very much regimented although not as much as Rehab treatment. For example, clients were not permitted to drive until they had progressed to a certain point. They were made to attend meetings and pushed to find employment. They were taught the basics of paying bills and other things that we had been doing for Z instead of allowing her to grow up. This sounded good to me, and I looked at my wife to see if we were on the same page. She asked some questions and then agreed.

Unlike the other clients, Z had a job (as a chef) waiting for her. Some days she didn't leave work until almost midnight and thus she would have no transportation available for her commute back to the facility. So, they agreed to allow her to have her car at the facility but that she could only use it to go to and from work. With this problem overcome, we went to the office and paid for her first month's rent with the understanding that this was a one-time deal and that future payments were for her to make.

There is a difference between enabling and helping. Let's say that your loved one has been "on a run" (actively using) for a year or longer and that they have been unemployed all that time and were living on the street. They then repent and enter into treatment.

After treatment, they decide to enter into sober living (rather than head back to the streets) which insurance will not pay for. So now you must either find a halfway facility willing to scholarship them or you would have to pay for a few weeks—perhaps more—with the hope that they will find employment within that time.

Success! They have found employment (still supposing here). Don't forget, they now have to wait a week or two for their first paycheck to arrive. Your choices are to allow them to play catch-up with their rent and starve for three or four weeks or to help them financially. Yes, there is a difference between helping and enabling. There is nothing wrong with assisting your loved one temporarily so that they can get a start on their journey; there is, however, something wrong if you continue to support them for a prolonged period of time while they watch television and send out for food (that would be enabling).

One should keep in mind that fresh out of treatment, your loved one may be in a position where they are forced to seek employment that pays considerably less than what they were prepared for. Perhaps they were an engineer or a government worker. It might be a prolonged period of time before they can once again find employment in their chosen field. You are *by no means obligated to support* them until they once again qualify for rehire. There is no shame in signing up for the labor force. It's an honest day's work for an honest day's pay. The sooner you stop paying, the sooner they will start. The less money that they are left with after expenses, the less chance of them thinking about using the excess for relapse.

The above examples could show both enabling or helping, depending. You are not enabling if you help your loved one get on their feet for a short period of time. They should and will be encouraged at the facility to seek employment. There are jobs available and they are supposed to take what is available. Once employed, they then have the ability to seek better employment. The test is to see how you feel. Guilt is one key and annoyance is a second. If you feel either or both of these about what you are doing for your loved one then there is a high probability that you are enabling. Support should last no more than a month.

Rocky Times

We left the facility feeling well. We had received a good report and she was in a good place. We accepted this as an auspicious beginning to a better future. At week's end she would move from one residence to another and could return to work. Although she hadn't mentioned any specific problems at work recently, I knew that if her complaints began to mount about how unfairly she was being treated at work, this was a sign that she was once again using. For now (and hopefully forever) she could resume her career, moving upward in the culinary profession.

Things went well for about a week and a half. Then she called, proclaiming that she was asked to leave the facility. Heart burn and nausea were becoming a way of life for me. I told her I was busy at work and would speak to her later. That I did, later that night. It seemed that one of her roommates had introduced Z to her brother, who was in treatment, and they had found love. The fact that this was totally against regulations had no effect upon my daughter's judgment. She was, after all, an adult and "quite capable of deciding who she could go out with and when."

I tried to explain that these regulations had not been created arbitrarily to make her life miserable and that there were proven, valid reasons for the rules and they should be adhered to. She would not hear of this and demanded to move back home with her new boyfriend. This was only partially okay with me. *She* could move home. *He* had to make other arrangements. Home she came with a car full of laundry and into her room she went. I decided to call the facility to find out what had actually occurred.

It seemed that she was secretly seeing this guy and they felt that she was on the verge of relapse. They offered to readmit her into the rehabilitation program if she was willing but she could not jeopardize the other resident's sobriety by remaining at the facility that she was in. I discussed this with Z and was met with a vitriolic barrage aimed at the facility and myself for not agreeing with her.

"Who the hell are they to tell me who I can see and when I can see them?" she insisted again. You can see the addictive personality is one that is capable of clear reasoning immediately after they are drug free. (This is sarcasm. If you don't believe this statement, ask any addict as they leave a treatment center and see if you trust their judgment or for that matter, ask the addict if they are ready to trust their own judgment.)

At this point I hoped what I was thinking was wrong, but I had a bad feeling about what the future held. My wife, however, was not so sure that my daughter was wrong. My knowledge of this disease at this time was also not as attuned as it is now so yes, I can admit that I was enabling my daughter by allowing her to return home.

By nature I am not antagonistic or pugilistic, yet since I do have a tendency to let my feelings be known on occasion, and sometimes not very nicely (back to Z's outburst), I just left the room and turned on the TV—now my recreational drug of choice.

After a time of watching in silence, my wife asked what was up. I kept silent because hostility, like drugs, distorts the thought process. On occasion release is necessary but rage has no positive effect and definitely no place in a rational discussion. The wisdom that I had been developing worked well when dealing with the clients at the treatment center and with my daughter when the therapist was there to control the conversation, but when in a one-on-one with her, sometimes the conversation digressed to a shouting match—and I was doing all I could to avoid an unnecessary eruption. (Should this occur, it is best to end the conversation and wait for a better time to try again.)

So I lowered my voice and told my wife what had transpired. She knew as well as I that my daughter didn't act as she just had unless she was in relapse mode. My daughter and wife both knew that *entering into a relationship is not recommended in early recovery*. This did not stop my wife from making a feeble defense on Z's behalf.

There are many reasons that the addict just out of treatment should not enter into a relationship. First and foremost, their attention should be devoted to working their program and staying straight. Second, their self-esteem is somewhere around a one or two out of ten, ten being the best. The significance of developing self-esteem may not even register with your loved one. According to my daughter, the rules were there to hinder her sobriety, not to help. Her thinking is not unique. Most addicts ready to relapse think in a similar manner. Giving into this thought process is a form of enabling, which every family member is guilty of at some time during the healing process.

Z, I found out, was a master in the art of manipulation. My wife was one who the manipulator could play like a Stradivarius violin. I was not free from being manipulated or from enabling. The difference was that I was a pharmacist and had had contact with addicts for many years and had experience with the process of manipulation. Plus, what I was learning at the Family Night meetings allowed me to see/understand when I had just been manipulated. Still, there is a difference between dealing with someone who is in early recovery versus someone in active addiction.

Z was back home and I knew this was not good. My wife spoke with her and agreed that the therapist that I spoke to on the telephone had no right to speak to me in the manner in which she did. The therapist should have been more encouraging and wished us luck. If I were an ostrich I would have buried my head in the sand. My wife is guilty of being an over-protective and loving mother. This has its place in the family arrangement but not in the recovery process. The therapist *was trying desperately to prevent a relapse*. If anything, she was guilty of having crummy conversational skills. She was abrupt and should have realized that when a family member is calling in crisis, her job is to get the point across in a firm but compassionate manner so that the already-stressed family member doesn't leave the conversation lost and angry. I have found that in the field of addiction treatment everyone is constantly learning.

Later that week I got to meet her boyfriend. He actually seemed to be a nice guy. They went into my office and investigated the list of halfway houses that they had found online. She found several that appealed to her. My wife and I went to check them out. Some were nice and others I wouldn't have slept in wearing a hazmat suit. She finally decided on one but when we checked it out it was cost prohibitive. So, it was back home for Z until such time that she found a place that she could afford.

Her boyfriend found a temporary place to stay and visited with her every day. I liked this about as much as I liked tight shoes, but she was working and still seemed to be straight so I figured maybe I would go along with the group. What I never thought to ask was how her new loved one was enjoying his new work experience. As it turned out any work experience was a new experience for him. Actually it was so new that he was still waiting to experience it. Actually, if there was something that could have *a more negative effect on his emotional thinking process worse than relapsing* it would have been to look for a job.

One day I came home from work and my wife told me that Z had found a facility where they could both live. I found this hard to believe but was promptly put in my place. This was a sober-living facility where they would be randomly drug tested and could go to meetings nightly. I thought maybe I was wrong but I always assumed that a halfway house had separate facilities for male and female clients. This was "a new kind of halfway house" I was told. I was told how antiquated the treatment center was in their thinking. This was the new way. If bullshit were a commodity all addicts would be wealthy. This I would later learn. The truth was that although I did attend the Family Night meetings once weekly and thought that I knew a little about this disease, *you never know enough*, especially when it comes to your own family member.

My wife and I went to check out the facility and found it livable. It was what she could afford and it looked clean and somewhat aesthetic. It was the first time she was going to be on her own and perhaps this was what she needed to develop a sense of responsibility. I approved although I did not like the idea that this new boyfriend was going to be living there also. He seemed nice enough but rough around the edges. Dealing with the public for as long I have has given me a sense of what people are about. As far as I could tell this guy was, at best, sitting on the fence. Time would be the great decider. Also, and I can only attribute this to my limited knowledge as well as my naïvety, I figured that if this was a sober-living facility that it must be licensed and legitimate.

My wife was in contact with my daughter more than I was. She used the excuse of working and going to NA meetings to avoid Family Night. I still attended and was able to discuss my thoughts and feelings to see if I was just a cranky old man or correct in my feelings. If you take the time to think things through in a rational manner before you react, you will probably do the right thing. To be sure, I would run my thoughts by the therapist who was so much help at this time that I can't begin to equate her with any prior experience in my decision-making processes. This could be due to the fact that she was the first therapist that I had worked with. However, it did seem that both the clients and the family members were impressed with her ability and I certainly was.

She too viewed Z's living situation askance. She knew of no legitimate facility that allowed for cohabitation at this early stage of recovery unless the couple had both gone into treatment at the same time and perhaps they were married or in a permanent relationship. Even those clients who were married and felt the need to go to halfway living did so alone. Perhaps they were able to arrange weekend passes but feeling the need for a more structured period after completion of the rehabilitation program, they usually chose to live in a halfway house, alone, to await visits from their husband or wife and family members. So now I had a daughter who had found a place that allowed her to cohabitate with her boyfriend…not to mention that both had been kicked out of their respective facilities. Not only did I not believe what I was hearing but I was afraid of the outcome and sensed an imminent relapse.

Unfortunately, I was the only one who felt this way at home. I expressed my feelings but to no avail. They moved into the so-called facility and there was nothing I could do. As you listen to sober addicts discuss their time while using, you will become more familiar with the excuses that they use to encourage enabling. Your loved one may say to you, "I have to pay for a course at the addiction college so that when I enter into treatment I will qualify as a technician. So do you think you could pay my rent this month?" Or perhaps, "I haven't eaten in a few days. Can you take me food shopping? You can pay the cashier so there is no worry that I will keep the money." They then wait for you, who feels like you have done something to help your loved one, to leave so they can return the groceries and use the money to buy drugs. Hopefully this example can aid you and your family members in avoiding the enabling trap that is so easy to get caught up in. Knowing that what you are going to do might have negative consequences should not stop you from proceeding with the action. The bond between a child and parent is unconditional. It is much stronger than the bond between siblings or spouses. This is good but can be dangerous as it has the potential to blind our judgement, allowing us to enable without realizing we are doing it. Maybe the safe thing to do would take them out to eat and you pay the bill. The meal is consumed and there is no chance for them to get the money. The plus is that they just had a good meal.

At first, things appeared to go well. I had little contact with Z as I was working and as she was too, our times did not coincide to allow us to interact. From what I heard from my wife, everything was going well. Ever the skeptic, I kept waiting for the ominous call, alerting us to disaster. With every ounce of fatherly love in me, I wanted things to go well. Every bit of knowledge that I had was banging me on the head, alerting me to the fact that this could and would not end well.

When your child is an adult, there is little you can do but offer love, advice, and most of all, make every effort not to enable them. This is a hard time for the family members. Every paternal or maternal instinct tells you to *help the addict*. Buy them a new wardrobe and bring them home and they will see the error of their ways if you just show them love and compassion. If this worked there would be no disease known as addiction. Most family members, especially those that are not addicts, love their addicted family members and spend their lifetimes trying to get them to see the error of their ways. Unfortunately this does not work. This is a disease that makes the advanced chemistry courses that I took in college seem like elementary school science. People have devoted their professional endeavors to "trying to understand" the addictive personality, without total success. One of the hardest things to figure out is what makes up their thinking process. You just have to wait for what *triggered the relapse to release its grip and for your loved one to hit bottom*. Then, hopefully, they will seek help. Hopefully this will occur before they harm themselves or someone else.

Well, my worries about Z's new residence were valid. My wife approached me one night to tell me that some of our daughter's things were missing from her room. I asked if it were possible that she and her boyfriend had sold them and were hoping that we would buy her replacements. This was met with a barrage of, "You always think negatively!" and, "How do you expect her to stay well if we always suspect her of relapsing?"

Well, it was late and I was tired, so I sat down on the couch, turned on the TV, and ate my supper. My wife spoke little to me for the next few days. Perhaps it was I who did the little speaking; who can remember when your life is consumed with work and aggravation? The calls from my daughter began to become more frequent. Her things were disappearing. I asked if she locked her door before leaving for work. She responded that there were no locks on the doors in case of an emergency. I responded that either one of the boarders living there or her boyfriend was taking her things and likely selling them. It was obvious that a resident was in active addiction and had to steal to support their habit. She admitted that the thought had crossed her mind although it had to be some other resident as she and her boyfriend were both going to meetings every night and most assuredly were straight. I told her to ask if she could buy a lock for her door and that I would come by on the weekend and install it for her. She immediately responded defensively, saying that if they gave them permission, her boyfriend could install the lock. The conversation was over.

I hung up the phone—the usual sick feeling was back. I knew that before long, trouble would surface even if now she was straight. The process of relapse almost always starts before the picking up of drugs occurs. The use of the drug itself is the final stage of relapse. It usually starts with, "I don't have to clean my room," or "I can't attend all those meetings as I work too hard," or "I'm tired, and I think I'll call in sick today." My daughter was no exception; she was not living the way she needed to if she was going to remain straight. I had a strong feeling that my worries of her relapsing "one day" were moot. I would have bet money that the relapse process had already begun. I knew my daughter would never admit to this so I had to wait until she continued along the downward spiral and hope that it didn't end in arrest or death. All that I felt that I could do was offer to pick her and her boyfriend up and take them to the Family Night meetings or into treatment. She knew that I attended these meetings weekly and perhaps she wouldn't take the offer as an act of rescue on my part as I'd been offering since she had completed her first treatment. The sure sign that a relapse had occurred with Z was when things suddenly started to go wrong yet it was never her fault: her boss is crazy and picks on her, someone backed up on a major highway, slammed into her car and drove away, the police found a vial of pills with her name on it but they weren't hers—she got them for the guy who was checking her oil on the highway when the car backed into her.

The farther into the relapse, the more outrageous the stories become, and the potential to believe them can actually increase if we are not educated about this disease. So now I had to play the waiting game. I would try to pry information from her when we spoke, but she avoided me, knowing well that I knew what was happening. Aside from encouraging your loved one to enter into treatment *you cannot be the savior.*

It was almost as though there was some collusion between my daughter and wife, for soon after things started disappearing from her room, she suddenly grew frightened to live at her residence because there were "fights occurring all the time." On the next Saturday, we came home from eating out, and the phone rang. It was Z. Someone had tried to steal something again and her boyfriend had a fight with this someone and there was some kind of catastrophe going on and please could we come and get them. His mother would pay us rent so that it would actually be like he was renting a room from us.

I said that I didn't want them moving into the house. If they were going to live together, which I was totally against, they would have to find their own place. First, why was his mother paying the rent? Why wasn't he working and paying his own rent? Second, I didn't need a boarder living with us, especially one that I didn't know—a recovering addict who had just gotten into a fight and seemed to have trouble finding work…and was most likely not in recovery but rather in early relapse phase if not in total relapse. I fought hard to keep them out of our home.

The New Boarders

Yup, you guessed right. I guess my foot was not heavy enough because as I pulled up to the so-called facility, there were the two kids packed and ready to come home with us. What was supposed to have been a little slice of a new beginning for addicts and a place for extra support to those new to recovery looked more like a snapshot from some grade B movie dealing with gangbangers: even the police were there. My heart sank as we pulled up to the so-called facility. The purpose of this trip was to *pick up our daughter* and bring her home but there was her boyfriend with all his (meager) belongings, sitting in the back of my SUV next to Z. My wife told me to shut up and drive as maybe the police might start to question why they were leaving. So off I went with a lot of dirty clothes and two pending disasters in the back seat.

Home I drove with many words upon my tongue that at that point, I could not yet spew forth. Was this my wife again enabling? Most assuredly! Was I too, to blame? Most assuredly! Is enabling part of this disease? As a bushy eye-browed comedian of yesteryear was famous for saying, "You bet your life." Did that make what we were doing all right? No. So how do you handle a situation like this? You attend Al-Anon meetings and seek help in dealing with life as an addict's family member or close friend.

So now my wife is sitting next to me, not thrilled to have him, but if it meant our daughter would be safe at home, she would live with it. (And enough dirty clothes to start a commercial laundry.) I was upset but something told me this was to be short-lived. Everything that I had learned had taught me that living with a family member in active addiction was a nearly impossible feat. Living with a stranger in active addiction made the feat not just impossible, but insane. I was sure that something would happen and, not me, but my wife would toss him out.

My wife swore that they were both straight. My heart wished for her to be right but my brain told me that the therapist I had spoken with was probably right on when she said relapse was about to happen. Still, for the sake of my sanity and to avoid strain on a long-term marriage, I went along with this supposedly temporary arrangement. The theory went something like this: "Our daughter is employed but her boyfriend is looking for a job. When he finds one, they will get an apartment and move out." As we know, not all theories are proved true.

Z would get up, dress in her chef attire, grab her mug of freshly brewed coffee (that my wife had prepared for her), and off to work she went. Around 10 am her boyfriend would begin to stir and then leave the room. He would open the garage door, stand out in front of the house and smoke a cigarette. He would then sit by my computer for about five minutes, claim there were no jobs today, retire to Z's room and watch TV and nap for the rest of the day. At least that's what he claimed to be doing and I, as the benevolent husband and father, chose to accept this "napping" for the moment. I would smile, wondering how long this would last before my wife's thoughts turned to eviction or the assassination of Z's boyfriend.

Surprisingly, it took several weeks. Into the bedroom my wife and I walked one night. We shut the door and then she began to vent. She was beside herself with rage as she spoke about how Z was "supporting him" and "he was making no pretense at finding a job."

Eventually, she asked me to speak with Z. I stared at her coldly. She had created and enabled this problem and now I was asked to try to straighten it out. I try to deal with problems in an intelligent manner at first. Sometimes a nice conversation can work things out. My wife, on the other hand, is excitable. Despite all this, I agreed.

When I explained to Z that we were not happy with the living situation, I spoke in a soft and pleasant way. I explained that they had been living with us for two weeks now, and he had not gone out looking for a job once. She claimed that it "was different times" and that you don't "go looking" for a job anymore. Instead you check the computer and send out resumes and then wait for a response. I mentioned that that seemed to be something that he was good at.

"What?" Z asked.

"Waiting for responses." The look I received was not a nice one. She then explained that it was especially hard for him to find employment because he had not yet gotten his license back. I paled at this newfound bit of information. I hadn't even thought to inquire as to whether or not he had a driver's license. I was sure that he was driving her car when they went out. My thoughts concerning these two could only be construed as naïve. What so-called knowledge of the disease of addiction did I have? A lesson to be learned is that just when you think you know about this disease, you get that humility kick in the butt that reminds you that you can never really understand it. The fact that *I was surprised* about this new bit of information was evidence of *how little I actually knew*.

All in all we had a pleasant conversation, while I politely yet firmly let her know that her mother and I were not at all pleased with the living arrangement and that Beau should start looking for another apartment. To me, it looked as though they were using again. Z agreed that they would look for an apartment or a sober-living residence as soon as he found a job. I then asked how he could ever hope to find a job unless they advertised on TV. I asked how she felt about working so hard as a chef while he lounged around all day not looking for work. She responded that he would eventually find something in the construction field as he was quite talented working with electricity.

I spoke with my wife about our conversation but she was still not happy. She wanted me to evict the boyfriend and keep the daughter. I tried to explain that from what I was seeing they were a team and would not be separated. She told me I was too nice and that she would speak to our daughter next time. I agreed that this would be a good thing and that since she had gotten us into this situation, maybe she could get us out of it.

When I came home late that night I was greeted in the living room by a face that showed both anger and disgust.

"What up?" I asked, exhausted from work.

"I can't take it anymore. I told Z that Beau is a no-good bum who will never work and is living off of her and us. I also asked her where the money was that his mother was supposed to be sending us for the food and rent." I looked at her askance. Did she really believe he would give us money when that money could be used to buy drugs? I asked her this and she replied that they were not using. Z had assured her that they were not using. When I asked when the last time was that they had gone to a meeting, she told me to ask Z.

"I bet that they no longer attend meetings and they have relapsed," I suggested.

"Do you know this for sure?" she asked.

"I haven't caught them using but I can tell by their actions that all is not well in Fantasy Land." I told her that her shouting did not make the situation any better and that sitting down and having an intelligent conversation would accomplish more. No, I am not a pushover. I just approach these problems in a more pragmatic manner. I told her that if she wanted to shout and fight, she could handle the situation…otherwise I would.

Actually, we were *both* living in la-la land. You cannot, as a somewhat rational person, hold a rational conversation with someone who is not in a rational state. By definition, when someone is in active phase of addiction, they are no longer capable of being rational. So by definition, we were both guilty of trying to do something that was undoable. At a time such as this you have to set a boundary and maintain it. You should tell them that they have until a certain date to vacate the premises and you then make sure that they are out on that date. If necessary, take them to a shelter, but they must vacate the premises or they will never respect what you say again. Of course, this is so much easier to say than do when you are the parent and have not yet reached the point of *compassion fatigue*.

Later that week my daughter came home with bad news. She had been suspended from her job for arguing with one of her supervisors. I told her that she had a car payment and other expenses coming due so she had better find a job fast—I knew that suspended was her euphemism for *fired*. The next morning, she got up early and searched online for chef jobs. Later that day she told us that she had sent out several resumes and was expecting to get a call for an interview soon. She then joined her boyfriend in her room and stayed there for the rest of the day.

My wife was very upset. Her job had not just been a good one—it also gave her health insurance as well as many other benefits which most chefs at the lower level don't ever dream of receiving. I knew that she was worried that if Z was using again and needed treatment, she would have to go through a county facility which is not nearly as nice as private pay. Perhaps this is what she needed. A taste of what real life was about. Maybe it was time to stop pampering her. I had heard that the county treatment facility was not so bad. They were county supported and had better-than-decent detoxification and rehabilitation programs.

I recommend checking out the facilities offered in your area before you decide that it doesn't measure up (to what your loved one's expectations are) and put yourself into debt. For the most part, most government facilities do not compare to the private ones, but the most important aspect of the success of a treatment center is your loved one's willingness to work their program and to receive help.

Years before I ever dreamed that a family member of mine would or could suffer from this disease, I attended fundraiser affairs for the county facility. The Booher Foundation would run these fundraisers, dinner functions attended by many, who would get to meet and greet many dignitaries, including elected officials, judges, and other attendees who knew of the work that this organization did to help those suffering from the disease of addiction to get the help they needed. This came to an abrupt halt when it was decided that we could not have fundraisers for a county facility. (You have to wonder to what extent the perception/lack of understanding about this disease goes.) Someone had to bring this out in the courts to determine that it was "improper." You would think that the only ones hurt by this victory were the addicts who benefited from these fundraisers but this was not true. This disease affects the whole community. It affects those who are upset when they see the people standing on the corner holding a sign begging for food, those who are accosted as they enter or leave a store by someone asking for money, and also by someone who is attacked by someone trying to get their next fix. This cannot be understood until someone gets to be the recipient of the residual effects of this disease or suddenly realizes that a loved one suffers from the disease.

The addict will find a way to get their drugs. Drugs costs money, so often when the disease progresses to the point where they can no longer legally provide an income for themselves, they are forced to provide this income in other-than-legal ways. These ways may seem insignificant at first. Perhaps just a tool is missing from your garage, or an earring made of gold seems to have mysteriously vanished. You never suspect that your family member would steal from you so you blame the gardener or the man who came into the house to fix something. You might not realize what is happening at all, or perhaps you refuse to realize what is happening.

Z had always been lucky enough to be able to find many jobs throughout her life. As previously mentioned, there are a lot of jobs out there for trained chefs willing to start at the bottom. Even if they have experience, restaurants try to start new-hire chefs in as low a position as they can get away with. When you're an addict and are looking for a job, you accept what is offered and don't argue about salary. Health benefits are a plus as you can use this to obtain drugs on prescription. She was able to get jobs; it was *keeping* them for any prolonged period of time that was the difficulty.

It seemed that when she started a new job she would either get clean for a while or use Suboxone, a narcotic antagonist/opiate combination that allows you feel high yet to function better than if using other drugs. It always amazed me how well she could do at the beginning, getting praise from her superiors and promises of promotions, only to be later suspended and then fired. This hurts family members more than the addict. When an addict is using, their senses are numbed by the drugs and they can't feel what they would normally feel (if sober) in response to a situation. Thus you will most likely feel worse that they got fired than they do. They may feel a certain amount of remorse, but this is more apt to be due to the fact that they no longer have cash flow coming in to support their need for drugs.

My sober thought process could not allow me to think in the pattern of the addicted person. I also, deep down inside me, refused to believe that my daughter had actually become an addict who had no control over her ability to think in a rational manner. I thought that I was pretty much aware of the situation. The reality is that a family member finds it very hard to comprehend that their loved one has reached this level. Z would come up with almost-believable excuses for the reason she was fired. Sometimes she would blame me for pushing her towards the culinary profession. At first I would accept the blame for her circumstances although I would never admit it. As I have mentioned, one of the most remarkable features of this disease is the ability of those addicted to manipulate their loved ones. To this effect, my daughter was a pro. This is why we needed help as much as Z did.

Don't be surprised when things start to disappear from the house. Be upset, sure, but surprised, nope. You're not likely to bring charges against your loved one, so they see you as a safe target. This is the way of the addict: just as you need air to breathe and food to eat, they need drugs to exist. They will get these drugs if they have to prostitute themselves or mug someone or burglarize a house. Whatever it takes, the addict will get their fix and there is no way that the family member (unless they too suffer from this disease) has a chance of understanding their actions. I have heard it explained as, "The need to use has replaced their survival mechanism." This disease knows no boundaries. Neither background, age, nor education level makes a difference: there are no differences when it concerns this illness. The only common denominator that applies is that *when they need to get high, they will*, no matter what it takes. The only people capable of setting boundaries and keeping them are the family members in sobriety.

So now I had not one but two unemployed addicts living in my house: one who had just lost her job and one who broke out in a rash if the word "work" happened to be mentioned in his presence. I am basically an agnostic but at that time found myself often looking skyward and asking what I had done to bring such a vengeful wrath upon me.

One day Z came into the TV room and announced that she had an interview with a catering service, left, then came home smiling. It was near the house and she would start the following week. There were no benefits, but the pay was close to what she had been making at her last job. My wife and I congratulated her. We refrained from asking her about her boyfriend who was too busy searching for a job to actually get one. I had recently seen him sleeping with the want ads over his head. Having worked summers since I was twelve years old, I could not understand, but that is the way of the severely enabled addict.

Having Z go to work while the love of her life slept all day was beginning to bring out the Lizzy Borden side of my wife's personality. A healthy male of his age sleeping all night and day was incomprehensible to her. I would come home from work and be greeted by tirades of how "…he just lies in bed," and, "How can she go out with a bum like him?" and, "When the hell are they going to move out?" To make matters worse, the money that was promised for room and board never made it to our hands. I told my wife that I suspected that they were both getting high and that we should have never taken them in. It's amazing how much easier it is to *take someone in than to get them out.*

Things were growing tenser each day until finally my wife started to lash out at him. Perhaps she could have handled him if he at least had made a pretense at seeking employment. This boy had no shame and nothing was going to budge him from the room. Finally, to silence my wife, he trudged into our computer room to look, once again, for employment opportunities. (I wondered if there were jobs available for mattress testing.) I seriously doubted that he was seeking employment of any kind.

His mother had previously supported him (and his addiction) and now my daughter had taken over and *we were helping her*. This situation is exactly what would appear on your computer screen if you Googled the word "enable." If you're unsure of whether you are enabling a family member versus loving them, consider this: once they reach a certain age, a family member should not be living with you, as this allows you to support their behavior. Another test is whether you feel any resentment for what you are doing for them. They need to learn to stand on their own two feet and this will never be accomplished if you continue to support them (even if they are not getting high).

One day I asked my daughter to meet me at work so I could speak with her privately. This opportunity was brief as I never have much spare time at work. I asked why this guy never looked for work and left her bedroom only to go outside and smoke. I asked how she could like a guy who had no intentions or the ability to support her. Her response was a sickening, "But I love him." I could only attribute this to her addictive behavior and very low self-esteem. I told her to think about how hard it is to exist in our society with only one income, especially when one of the supposed breadwinners stays home and lies in bed all day (I could only assume at this point) getting high. She promised to talk with him later. I was upset though, as I knew that to the addicted mind what I had just said meant nothing more than, "Dad is trying to stop me from scoring on the way home so I can't get high in my room with my true love."

You think you are doing the right thing, but as you learn more, you begin to realize that what you *are* doing is exactly what you *shouldn't be* doing. Until you have reached the point of *compassion fatigue,* it is very hard to throw your loved one out of your house, knowing that they will most likely spend a few nights on the street. What is compassion fatigue and when does it hit? It depends on the individual. It is the feeling you get when, no matter how many treatments or incarcerations have occurred or how many things are stolen from your house, you finally have the feeling that you can *no longer take or put up with* the emotional turmoil that your loved one puts you through as a result of their addiction. This gives you the courage to do what is necessary, kind of a survival mechanism, to change your situation so that you can survive. It made me stop going to court with my daughter. I told her she could no longer live at home and get high, she could no longer visit if she was high (boundaries). These were things that I could never say or do, initially. Does it hurt to do these things? You bet! It also feels good as you are being set free from living in hell.

So they continued to live with us, sharing a room together, rent free, likely both using, and using the monies saved from my enabling to support their habit. To make matters worse, my supposed "rent money" and my daughter's hard work were paying the way for this guy to sleep, smoke, and indulge in the world of the addict.

At the meetings I attended I would often speak of the negativity of enabling, and here I was wearing the crown as the king of all-time enablers. I knew that something had to be done soon. It was bad enough that I was allowing my daughter to live at home free of charge but now I was stuck with the love of her life as my new dependent. Not only was I living with the guilt of knowing that I was doing something wrong, I also felt weak for not having the ability to end it. One should never have to live with these feelings just because their loved ones have developed the skills to manipulate them. It is bad enough when you are new and still don't comprehend the reality of what you are doing, but in my instance, I *knew the reality* so my feelings were multiplied.

The problem rectified itself with the aid of my wife. Whoever claimed that man is dominant was definitely a chauvinist. I have found that women can be the more aggressive of the sexes and my wife was proof. Here's what happened: one day Beau pushed the cart too far and my wife exploded. She screamed at them and things got pretty ugly. When I came home from work, she told me the story and though I felt miserable, I agreed. It would not be easy to tell them to leave. It was against parental instinct to give Z the boot.

Much to my surprise and relief, when Z returned from work that night she said that they would be moving out. She knew how we felt and didn't want us to have ill feelings toward him so felt it would be best if they moved. Ill feelings are the body's natural response to being abused by someone and that is exactly what your loved one is doing to you when they move into your home and allow you to support them and their habit. We accepted the news gleefully. This unbelievable turn of events took the pressure off of me and we avoided a conflict that would have been ugly and likely would have accomplished nothing other than my wife and I being upset. When someone in active addiction is asked to do something such as get their own apartment, most often the result will be in your favor. They can look for a place to live for eternity or until a better situation presents itself. When you see their alternative to living with you, you will probably regret having asked them to leave.

Supporting an addict—enabling them—is wrong. It is an easy statement to make but hard to take action against. Rendering a loved one homeless is heartbreaking. We are told that enabling can result in the death of the addict. This is similar to how we feel about someone smoking. We know that smoking can result in death but it's not imminent. Same thing with the concept of an overdose. We know that it can happen "one day" but we don't see it happening anytime soon to our loved one. At first. As the disease progresses, the family develops a fear of their loved one overdosing and dying. You have to be strong and do your best to act appropriately as the end result of this disease is not a pretty one. For this reason I once again stress the need for you, the family member, to attend the meetings. They can save you, your marriage, and your loved one. There are no right answers—making this disease so complicated.

There are families that feel that keeping their loved ones at home is safer than forcing them out onto the street. If they overdose and die in the house they blame themselves for the death. Then there are those that send their loved ones out and if they overdose and pass away, they still blame themselves for the choice that they made. My feeling is that if you give someone a place to live, food and clothes, and a nice car to ride around in, (and all the while know they are getting high) what on earth would be their incentive to enter into treatment? My advice is to do what you feel is right, aside from enabling your loved one, and hope for the best as there are no right answers where this disease is concerned.

I Have My Home Back

Z found a "sober-living facility," with an inexpensive room available right away. I gave them my best wishes and out they went. Relief was the first emotion and lasted only until the euphoric feeling of having our home back wore off. Then no euphoria turned into the familiar feelings of worry. Thankfully, Z still felt intimidated enough by her parents to try to hide the drug use, so she called every day or so and tried to act and speak as though she were still sober. The addict is cunning and knows how to control their high. For example, if they know they are going to call you or visit on Monday they use enough drugs to stay level. This allows them to sound and act straight without getting *dope sick*. Dope sick is the term to designate the feeling that the addict gets when they are in need of a drug and have started to enter into withdrawal. They may have cramps, diarrhea, nausea, aches, pain, and/or seizures.

It was good to hear from her to know that she was safe. I was living a somewhat normal life at this point, allowing myself to feel that possibly my daughter was doing okay. Even if she did have this parasite living off his parents and her, she was working and living on her own. The good thing was, although I knew what was happening, it was not happening in front of me. You will find that it is often hard enough to control your own thought process: you cannot control the thought process of someone in active addiction.

One of the hardest concepts to grasp is that *you do not have any control over the addict's thought process.* Neither threats, arrests, trying to show compassion, empathy, nor love will be accepted for what it is if the need to enter into treatment is in any way associated. The exception to this is if the addict decides to enter into treatment on their own.

I now had to hope that this arrangement was going to last for a while. I knew enough that the chance of this happening was not great. I also knew that the so-called sober-living facility was probably a flop house. Their accreditation should be scrutinized as most facilities do not recommend dating or cohabitation for a period of time. Remember my previous words that those in recovery should not date until their self-esteem has elevated to a level of eight—"Don't date till you're an eight"? And how do they know when that point is reached? "When they no longer have to ask." This is an indeterminant amount of time. It depends upon the person suffering from the disease. It is usually recommended that they wait about a year but that varies depending on how their program progresses.

Science is a wonderful area of academia and is mostly logical—the exception being the science of addiction. The non-addicted mind cannot comprehend the thinking mechanism of the addict. I have heard it explained that the serotonin and dopamine levels are altered in the brain and this can never reverse itself. Though I don't know if this is true, I do know that whatever changes do happen in the brain don't seem to revert back to normal and thus the addict can relapse at any time. I hoped for a recovery for my daughter as she sounded straight when we spoke but I knew that the odds were not in my favor. Still, you continue to hope and you continue to love.

I once heard the parent of an addict ask the group, "Why, after finally getting clean and accumulating an extended period of 'straight time,' would you possibly relapse, knowing what you are giving up and going back to? I just can't understand why after doing so well you would wreck everything and go out and use again." The answer that the addicts gave was startling for the parent. The reply was, "You can't understand this because you were never an addict." I too had to try to understand the enormous urge Z felt to use, *knowing that I could never understand it*. I suspected that these urges were what controlled her life and I hoped that she would be able to take control before she either ended up in jail or dead. I have heard it said that fighting the urge is a part of recovery and relapse is a part of the disease. To succeed and obtain long-term sobriety you must learn to control both. It is this need for control that creates the necessity of passionately working a program.

My daughter only told me good things. But I knew that she was living in a bad area of town where drug use and dealing were rampant. Unfortunately, this is where most facilities are located. You can listen to all the horse droppings that the politicos throw out to the public about trying to fight the war on drugs but try to open a facility in your city and see what it will cost just to cut through the red tape to get the zoning board to approve your request. It is much easier to open a medical office and turn it into a pill mill than to open a facility trying to help rehabilitate the addict. Bad areas can be a constructive part of the rehabilitation process. This is especially true for the new addict who comes from the *burbs* and mom and dad always did everything and protected them from the real world. It's scary out there and a reality check just might make them think about beginning the process of getting sober.

I was rapidly finding out that the longer my daughter used, the more distorted her thinking process became. This is not unique to Z. Addiction is a progressive disease. As sober parents (and not all parents are sober) we get more and more distraught trying to figure out what makes them behave the way they do. When they are straight and in rehab they think in a much more rational way that can allow us to again identify with our family member. It's sad when they relapse and they get taken away from us again.

It didn't take long for my wife's motherly instinct to once again raise its head. After a period of time my daughter once again began to complain about her living conditions. When my wife mentioned this to me I recognized the pattern and started my response with, "NO…" But she laughed and said, "No way can they move in with us again." This made me worry as I knew that in my wife's world "never" meant "at least for a few days." She was a mother and very permissive, and often this permissiveness is confused with being a loving mother. Each night I would come home from work or a meeting and catch a little jab about how she hoped our little darling was safe and that she had not picked anything up from one of the "medicinal sales personnel" who worked the streets in her neighborhood. In my facetious mind I wondered if my wife would have been as concerned if Z and Beau lived next door to a pill mill.

I mention this to point out the twisted thought process of the populace at the time. A doctor is a doctor and a pusher is a pusher and that diploma still protects the educated and prosperous in our mind, even though he has created more addicts and acted more the part of the pusher than the street thug selling dope. Even now that the authorities have finally cracked down on these doctors, one must admit that most middle-and-upper-class heroin addicts got their start at these doctor's pill mills.

Heroin has long been available to anyone willing to travel into the inner city to buy it. It was considered epidemic for the low-income inhabitants living in the ghettos, and nobody cared as long as it didn't hit the more affluent neighborhoods. Well, then it did and the government was forced to make a show of intervention. At the time this book was written, they have done exactly that: they have made a show of trying to rein in the legal pushers but they haven't done such a good job of it. If members of the recovery community were running the show, it would be much more effective as they have the knowledge to know what to do.

I interjected those thoughts to prolong the inevitable. One Sunday when I was off from work we had the kids over for a visit. The visit went well, meaning I was able to look like I was listening to the conversation of how they lived in constant fear of getting robbed or beaten up. I was alternating between half listening and not listening (but looking attentive) when I noticed that it was way past the usual time for them to leave. When I motioned for my wife to follow me into the bedroom she told me that they were scared to go home so she had told them they could stay. Apparently their television set had "been stolen" and my daughter slept with her computer in bed with her. I asked my wife if she was crazy.

"You almost had a nervous breakdown the last time they moved in and we had a hard time getting them out!" That was not even two months ago, and now here she was, resurrecting the situation again. How many times did this have to reoccur before she realized that we couldn't live that way? It was out of my hands and I was back to the pleasure of two addicts living with me. When you have an addict(s) living with you, there is a constant fear that your life might end, that your possessions will disappear, or that you will enter into their room to find them overdosed and now you have dead people in your home. It is a nauseating truth that family members of an addict have to come to terms with.

Life at home had now been reduced to sleeping with my jewelry on, bedroom door locked, and constantly listening at their door to hear if they were still moving and alive (all the while, they are denying that they are getting high). I sat on the couch at night and wondered what could possibly be the attraction to the intoxication? How could it create a mindset that has no consideration of its effect on their lives or the lives of their family members? Most importantly, how can they not see that each time they use it brings them closer to the edge of death? These questions, I am told, can only be answered by the addict and should not be attempted by the straight individual. It makes no sense to us. Our job is to do what we can to aid and abet in the healing process without enabling and to remember that they are our loved ones.

It didn't take long for the new boarders to find the minutest of my wife's exposed nerves. Perhaps this is a flaw or maybe I'm the one with the flaw as I have the ability to stay calm in situations that are not changeable without destroying relationships. Sometimes I wish I could react in a more aggressive manner. Usually, I first figure out what to do and then react, as opposed to my wife who first explodes, only to have a change of heart a short ways down the road. Perhaps we're both right—classic good cop, bad cop scenario.

She began to grow agitated after about three days, watching Z get up early for work and then watching Beau sleep until noon when he then had his first cigarette (that Z had supplied as he had no money: a common result of not working). The days passed with skirmishes between my wife and Beau occurring more and more frequently. She didn't complain to me as she knew that I wanted no part of this situation that she had created. I knew that the festering would eventually come to a head, just as a painful boil does, and I would somehow have the honor of being asked to lance it. I dreaded the thought of that day. I do have a temper and I knew that when the time came for it to awaken, it would not be pretty.

Life continued with feelings of total family dysfunctionality, my wife growing more regretful each day. I soon began to notice signs of relapse. When addicts try to cover up the fact that they are in relapse, they can be brilliant. That is why most people in the field agree that addicts are basically intelligent people. This is the hardest time for the family to understand this disease and why evicting your loved one can become essential.

The actions of the addict (towards their family) are part of the disease. The truth is they
will say and do *anything necessary* to get their drugs. This will include stealing your jewelry, television, or anything else that may bring in enough money to "get fixed." At this time their only thought or consideration is to get the drug. The problem is that until there is an explosion, the denial continues. The time comes that you catch them doing something that they can no longer deny that they were the one who did it. This is devastating to the family as usually they have been in denial—now this is no longer possible. So what do you do? There is nothing you can do except keep offering help in the way of treatment and stop enabling by offering money and lodging. This can be easier said than done and at that time, my wife and I were yet again both guilty of enabling. You will often hear the phrase "they must first reach their bottom before they will want to get help." Knowing where that bottom is is not something that is easily figured out, and it can change with each relapse. Every addict has their own bottom and this just may be death for some. Helping them by paying bills or allowing them to live with you may seem to be giving help, but you are in fact freeing up money for them to buy drugs. Try to think

how you lived when you went out on your own and allow them to live their life.

I knew that I was acting in an improper way which was half the battle. I did feel that at any time there would be an explosion and the situation would rectify itself. I was willing to play the waiting game as I felt this would remedy the addict situation as well as the wife problem. In the meantime, life was not getting better, and as I was also not getting younger, I would frequently wonder when my time to enjoy life would begin. I had been working hard since I was twelve years old and still worked full time when many of my friends were retiring. I saw no retirement for me in the near future and to add to my dismay, I had more than my share of aggravation at home. It was definitely time to attend Al-Anon again and thank God for my cousin's boyfriend who attended meetings with me and who also explained the ways of life in my situation.

They say it takes at least six Al-Anon meetings before you realize how the fellowship functions and how it affects you. This is true. I had enough experience to realize that I didn't have to live this way and that I could benefit from Al-Anon so I attended a few meetings but felt better attending NA and Family Night meetings at the treatment center. Al-Anon is a great place to go for help but it is not for everyone. I found that it was not my cup of tea as I could not bring myself to do the things that they recommended. Family Night was more to my liking, based upon my personal preferences, you may find them to be beneficial. Just give one a try and if it is not to your liking try another meeting—not all meetings are the same. There are many factors involved in deciding to attend these meetings. Check out the members. Do you find them to be to your liking? See how the meetings are run. Do you feel comfortable with the way the meetings are run? You should keep an open mind and remember the purpose of the meeting is to provide aid to the families of those that suffer from the disease.

Everyone reacts differently. For me, knowing that what I was experiencing was normal for someone who had allowed themselves to be manipulated into this position was soothing enough. My daughter and Beau, at that point, cared only about having a place to live and a meal so that they could get high. This was not my daughter and most likely his parents felt that this was not their son. I can safely make the assumption that we both spoiled our children, but there are many spoiled children who do not become addicts. These are unique times, when drug use becomes the norm, and we have to hope that our children get through this period without permanent residuals. The fact that there is a drug epidemic does not make using right. It does, however, bring forth more people for you to interact and to share your thoughts with.

Living conditions in our home continued to decline until one day my wife and I went shopping. On the return trip my wife seemed more upset than usual. She said that she thought she saw Beau in the process of injecting something. I told her that I was not surprised as I suspected that they'd been using for a long time. We returned home to find our two boarders on the driveway in the midst of verbally assaulting one another—Z was clearly high. This was not a normal argument but was a savage exchange of warlike profanities. Perhaps the hitting had already occurred but stopped when we pulled up. It was totally embarrassing as the fighting and language was taking place on my driveway where my neighbors could see and hear. I had somewhat of a meticulous reputation in the neighborhood both as a healthcare professional and as a political activist. I was known to be refined and educated: so I yelled at them to shut up and get into the house. My daughter refused to shut up.

Once inside, she showed me her bruised arm, claiming that he had abused her and that I should call the police. Beau showed me marks on him that he claimed she had caused. At this point I didn't know whether to call the police or just throw them out. I knew that if I called the police they would both get arrested and then when I calmed down I would have to deal with my wife, the legal aspects of the situation, and the guilt of having my daughter arrested. I also felt that this might devastate his parents. I had spoken with his mother on occasion and she was a decent woman who owned a business and loved her son.

Parents never want to have their child arrested, much less to watch them being arrested. I could feel the pressure rising up inside of me. By nature I am a quiet person who, most do not realize, has a bad temper. I tried to keep myself in control, but suddenly, I noticed things that used to be located on my daughter's dresser were now flying towards the wall. I also heard my wife's voice off in the distance shouting my name and telling me to stop and calm down. I didn't know if she was yelling out of fear that she would have to redo the walls or that I might have another stroke.

I then turned to the two kids and told them that I had already had one stroke and I wasn't going to have a heart attack also: they had to leave. My daughter left me with Beau, something she would never have done if she were straight. My initial thought was, *now what?* I asked him if he wanted to go back home. He did. He called his mother who told him he was high and thus not welcome. If he came home she would have him arrested. I knew what she was saying was right but I didn't want him there and felt it would be better for my daughter if he left. They were hindering each other's chance at sobriety. There's that codependency word again. I now understood the concept of why there should be no relationships for at least a year. If I had any previous doubts about the legitimacy of the idea, they were now gone.

I told him to pack his belongings and I would drive him to the airport. He told me he could not afford a ticket. I told him to call his mother or father again. He did and I could hear the shouting match that ensued. I decided that what was best for both him and my daughter was the separation that could only come by his returning back up north. I asked again if he wanted to return home and again his response was yes. He mother sent me a text, telling me to take him to a shelter. She was not going to take back a son in active addiction. I felt for her but I had my own problems with Z and I didn't need to adopt her son's problems too. I truly felt bad for him but the only alternative for him was to reenter treatment and get straight. If he really loved my daughter this was doable. At this point however, the only doable thing for me was to get him away from her.

I told him I would buy him a train ticket home. He agreed. His mother was upset. She had obviously seen too many relapses.

Deciding not to take an addict in when they are in active phase, is tough. Taking them in would be counterproductive for both the addict and the family member. It hinders the addict's decision to get help. Probably the correct thing for me to do would have been to call the police to arrest them both. But even when you *know* what the best choice is, it is not always easy to *do it*.

The feeling that develops when a person's loved one falls into a pattern of relapse and self-destruction can only be described as compassion fatigue. We get our hopes up (repeatedly) for a sustained recovery, only to have our loved one once again relapse. After several occurrences we're mentally and emotionally exhausted and start to vent in a manner that exhibits a lack of compassion toward our loved one. Next, we break off all external expressions of love and/or support for them. We may even become verbally abusive towards them. Family Night meetings can help you realize that despite this rebellion you *do still care*. With time and effort (on the part of the client) leading to a more successful recovery, you too will usually recover from this type of fatigue. My suggestion is working with a group such as one of the -Anons or a therapist may speed the healing process. You should not blame yourself for breaking off your relationship with your loved one at this time. If anything, blame yourself for not comprehending that when in active addiction, your loved one is totally irrational. It is normal that you get more and more aggravated when they react in a psychotic manner when you are waiting for/expecting a logical response. Again, if your loved one ever enters into recovery phase, with the help of a good therapist, they will come back to you.

If your addict is your spouse, you have added option of the dissolution of your marriage. Divorce is common. As a parent of a street addict I can appreciate those feelings. Living with an addict who frequently relapses is at best an unsatisfactory way to live your life. It would almost be easier if I could divorce Z. A parent, however, is always a parent, even if the addicted child chooses to go on a run and disappear for years—a parent's thoughts are always with their child.

There are those who choose to live with it, but it is also understandable when someone chooses to terminate their relationship.

A child can choose to disown a parent and a spouse can choose to terminate a marriage, for example.

So, my daughter's true love packed his bag and loaded it into the back of my car. On the way to the Amtrak station I asked if he had money to buy food for the trip home. He said he had no money at all. I could tell that he was high but still, I had a conscience. No one should go hungry. My wife was already looking at me, knowing I was going to buy food for him. I stopped at a fast food place and bought him enough to get him home.

Coming from Brooklyn, I felt a little uncomfortable facing forward with a rather distraught, totally intoxicated addict behind me. I kept checking the rearview mirror. He had always been a polite guy who had obviously had a proper upbringing then got caught up in the world of addiction—a world from which there is no return. The disease can be controlled but never cured and the addict's actions while in active addiction are never to be trusted—a lesson I was about to learn.

We reached the train station—of course, the train had left an hour ago. The next train was not leaving until the next day. I bought the ticket and was going to leave him at the station when the attendant told us that he could not wait there as the station closed at a certain time. I decided to get him a room in a motel next to the station so he could walk to the train the next morning. Call me dummy.

I should have taken his cell phone and mailed it to his mother but I was still naïve and uninformed. I told him not to call Z as she was high also and together they would most likely end up in jail. He took my advice—up until we were out of sight. I think it was about an hour after I returned home when I got the text from Beau that read Ha, I'm with your daughter, we cashed in the ticket, we're eating the food so how's that grab you? I was tempted to return to the hotel but I called the front desk instead. They said that a girl showed up, created a scene, and they threw them both out.

I learned two lessons that day. First, I should have bought a plane ticket, waited for him to board, and watched the plane take off. Second, if I had chosen not to buy a ticket, I should have listened to his mother and taken him to a shelter. The only other options were having him arrested or taking him to treatment. They will get their drugs and they will survive (if they don't overdose or manage to get themselves killed). They will get their way. It is very hard to outsmart them.

I was extremely upset about the text message and still am to this day. The positive side though is that I did vacate them from the house and I learned more about addictive behavior. The latter being a must for the family member of the addict. Until you learn about the manipulation and deception (and even after you have), they will continue to play you like a fiddle. This is not something that you should be ashamed of. It can be compared to a novice being lost in the woods versus a survivalist. The novice would starve and the survivalist would know exactly what to do to survive. The addict quickly develops the instincts to survive in active addiction and you don't require these instincts. So *don't ever expect to have the cunning acuity* that your addict has. Just be aware that they will use this ability to get what they want.

You should, however, keep in mind that no matter what they do, they do love you, and when they get straight they will be remorseful (beyond any of your expectations) for what they have done to you and your family. So don't take the actions of someone in active addiction as a personal assault or an act of hatred. *It is the disease acting.* They do not hate you. The guilt and shame they feel for what they have done to their loved ones is what often leads to the next relapse. Don't underestimate the importance of forgiving and moving forward when they are in treatment. Looking forward is part of the healing process. Looking back and holding onto resentment is often a cause for relapse.

Z and Beau were on a run for a few days. Then he went into treatment again, and she went "somewhere." The story she told me about staying at a friend's may be true, but who knows where she was staying? Perhaps she was sleeping in her car. Truthfully, I don't know. About a week later, we heard from her. She called my wife and asked if she could move back home. My wife said that it would be okay, but Beau was no longer welcome in the house.

The House Is Ours Again

Truthfully, I had missed having Z at home. After flare ups that result in a move out, your mind plays these little tricks on you. You kind of forget the bad times and remember the good. This is the way the brain works. You just got a little insight into the complexity of this disease, but it's quickly forgotten. Not only does your loved one act in a deceiving and cunning manner, so too does your own thinking process as it allows you to enter into a world of undeserved guilt.

Those of you who speak so fondly of your time in the armed services can do so because of this little trick our brains play on us. If we try hard we can remember how difficult the adjustment period was: while in basic training your sergeants took you to the brink of breaking and then slowly built you back up until you were ready for service. Basic training was hell but we forget just how hellish it was. The same goes for women who go through the pains of labor during child birth. Would you have had any more children if the pain that you bore during this time had not faded from your memory? One tends to mainly retain the wondrous feeling of seeing their baby emerge and of holding him or her to their chest—the beginning of the bonding process. The memories of the trauma that was inflicted upon you by your family member (especially if they are a child) fades once a period of time has passed. Addiction professionals will tell you to let them go.

Now my wife and I had an empty house as my other daughter no longer lived at home…but she was asking to. My head told me no. My heart told me yes. I had no idea where she was living and was fearful of her overdosing and ending up dead in some dump of a motel or in her car.

Z knew that I had some knowledge of the disease so she would call while I was at work and speak to my wife. I guess she figured she could work my wife easier than me. To tell you the truth, it was nicer now at home. The fright was still constant but not as stressful as getting up each morning and opening up her door, wondering if she was still breathing. I was now attending NA meetings regularly with a friend. Everything I learned from the NA and Family Night meetings taught me to offer support if she wanted to get help and to let her go and be on her own if she wanted to get high.

She called my wife one day and told her she was straight. She had used Suboxone to get off the heroin and had had a few weeks clean time. My wife believed this and told her she could come home, but alone. Beau was not ever welcome in the house again. I went along with this since we all talk the talk but when it comes to our children it is hard to walk the walk. Memories of how they used to be before being an addict constantly enter into our mind and it becomes easier to relent than to fight. Even if your loved one doesn't realize what the reasoning is, they know that there is something there that they can use to manipulate their family.

So back in she moved and the search for a new job began. She landed one in a few days and was back to being a chef. As usual, she excelled at her craft. After only a few months she was told that she was in line for a promotion. I was happy but not excited for this was part of her pattern. She excels, gets in line for a promotion, and then relapses. I never knew whether to be happy with her accomplishments or to begin preparations for the new wave of aggravation that inevitably followed. Being a parent, I opted to accept the praise she received and then hope for the best. At this time, I didn't quite believe she was straight. Getting straight is not an easy task, especially when your drug of choice is many. She initially started using alprazolam (Xanax), a benzodiazepine, (referred to as Benzos or Bars on the street and in the fellowships) so I had the feeling that if she did get off heroin she was still using this drug since detoxing from it is difficult—a process not easily done without professional help. It is also possible to hide the effects of this drug more easily than heroin's. I therefore figured that since they drug tested her prior to hiring, they probably had no inclination of her using the alprazolam. Or perhaps she did test positive for the alprazolam but had a legal prescription for it—more probable as they do test for benzodiazepines. Since she was still using this form of intoxicant, at any time she could again use heroin. It's impossible not to relapse when you're never totally sober.

Still, she worked and was able to pay her bills. The drama of when her boyfriend was living with us was over and the house again felt like I owned it. I didn't have to feel funny discussing things with her because he might overhear. I could argue with my wife in peace once again. Most important, and this might sound a little insane, I only had to worry about one child overdosing. I figured that someone else should have the honor of worrying about Beau.

Try as I might, I could never seem to get her to attend either AA or NA meetings. This is a significant step in the healing process and not attending is considered a prelude to a relapse. Going to meetings and having a sponsor are two basic requirements for a successful recovery. No legitimate sponsor will allow a sponsee (one who is affiliated with the sponsor in the fellowship) to use any type of intoxicant. I bring this up because my daughter tried to convince me that her sponsor had told her that Suboxone was okay to use in the recovery process. This is not true. At the time, Suboxone was used only as a *method of detoxification in the program*. Now there are facilities that allow what is known as Suboxone maintenance for those who are chronic relapsers.

Today, the significant increase in overdoses resulting in death has caused professionals to come to the conclusion that Suboxone maintenance is better than the possibility of relapse and a potential lethal overdose. I personally disagree with this but I am not an addiction professional so I defer to those who may know better.

It is not that I am a purist; Suboxone has a strong potential for abuse, both by the patient and by the doctors who provide the prescription for it. Another drug now used in this capacity is marijuana. Medical marijuana has its place in the treatment of certain illnesses but I feel that addiction is not one of them. I feel there is too much room for abuse and the potency is not governmentally controlled. It is still on the Schedule I drug list which makes it an illegal substance federally. Thus its procurement must be through a non-professional source. There is a place for this medication: seizure disorders or chronic nausea or pain.

As bad as it is living with an addict, only living with *two* addicts can show you how good it feels to have only your own again. I noticed several white tags on her key chain that they give out at the NA meetings, the tags you get for attending and showing a desire to stay sober. What I didn't see was a tag for thirty days or more. This meant that she had never gone more than thirty consecutive days without getting high. I often confronted her about this and her response was that I was never trusting of her. She felt that these meeting were not necessary and that since she worked so hard she could not attend them anyway. This too I found out was horse droppings. There are always places that you can go to attend a meeting, whether in the morning or evening. The fellowships are there to help addicts and they will work to do so, usually more than the addict will themself. The meetings serve to act as an aid for the addict who has a desire to maintain their sobriety.

Z was behaving at home and life was easier. The job was going well, she was speaking coherently, and my wife was happy. I suspected that she was using, but I couldn't get her to reenter a program. Although I was not totally happy about the situation, I was able to come home after a fourteen-hour shift, eat, and relax. When you have someone with this disease living at home you learn to take what you can and enjoy the better times as these don't usually last that long.

The Concept of "Normal"

Home life had once again returned to a state of normal. Hadn't it? As I thought back, I asked myself, *what is normal?* We have four daughters, so right away my concept of normal is perhaps a little askew. Each person has their own set of circumstances and I grew up thinking in one direction, my wife in another, and the children in their own, too. Ask any of us who was normal and we would each swear it was ourselves. The strange thing is we are probably all right.

Getting through life is tough, no matter how rich or poor you might be, although you can do more things if you are rich. The only thing that I am sure about is that you cannot go through life living as an addict. So if your addicted family member tells you that they are happy and that you should leave them to live their lives according to their norm you should be aware that it is the drugs talking. You cannot exist as an addict for any length of time, living any type of normal life. The disease is progressive and sooner or later they have to resort to some type of illegal activity to obtain the funds to support their habit (unless someone decides to enable their addiction).

My daughter was no exception. When she was in between jobs working as a chef, she worked at odd jobs and I mean they were *odd*. One job she claimed was that of a waitress. This seemed okay to my wife until I expressed the thought that I had never heard of a waitressing job that didn't require you to show up unless you felt like it. I figured that this "waitress job" just might be that of a dancer or worse. When I questioned her about the late hours of this server job and how she could just work when she wanted without calling in, she claimed that she was friends with the owner so he didn't care. This made no sense to me or, eventually, to my wife. My daughter saw nothing wrong with what she was doing so I would classify this as *Active Addiction's Normal*. The thinking process of one who is in active addiction is not rational. Generally, those considered capable of rational thought would agree, for example, on concepts such as what is and isn't legal. Most also understand that two plus two equals four but the addict's answer might be 150, and no matter what you say, you cannot convince them that they're wrong.

My wife loved my daughter unconditionally and would do anything to keep her happy. This included filling her car with gas, paying her insurance, and basically enabling her to keep a sense of normalcy in her life. She believed every story that my daughter put forth. When Z needed new chef attire, my wife would purchase it for her, stating that "it's for work so it had to be done." This would almost sound logical but she was living at home, not paying rent or expenses, so where was her money going? Her only expenses were her car loan ($300), insurance ($250), and her student loan ($100) for a total of $650. Her income was $1600 per month. So, where was the other almost $1000? My wife would then come to her aid, saying that she didn't want to put pressure on her or she might relapse. This I would classify as a *Loving Mother's Normal*.

Her sisters truly loved Z, but sometimes I got the impression they were upset by all the attention given to her. None of them are perfect but what is perfect? They do, however, work hard and support themselves and in return they receive *less from us than the addicted daughter does*. Is it not fair for them to react in a somewhat aggressive manner toward her? I feel that their behavior is inappropriate. Although I do see their point of view, I feel that they are more than a few years older than her and should have developed a level of maturity that would allow them to understand that it is her disease that is creating the aggressive feeling they have festering within them. So why then do they have these resentful feelings toward their sister?

This is hard for me to figure out, as my sister and I have always felt that we had to share and help each other. But, we never had to deal with this disease, so to be truthful, we actually don't know how either of us would respond if we did have to. I know that my other daughters know little of the intricacies of this disease and therefore must resent their sister and wonder why she is being rewarded for bad behavior. Perhaps they are correct as again we have to toe that microscopic line between helping and enabling. They see someone who is doing something wrong and being rewarded for it. They are right. They too could use the extra help but there is never enough to go around; thus the resentful feelings.

Their frustration is not wrong. To Z's siblings it seems that the more bad that she does, the better her treatment is. As you will see later, my wife and I eventually do set boundaries and stop treating Z with rewards for her negative behavior. This is something that comes with time and you have to work at your own pace. Ideally, you want to do this with a minimum of guilt and enough strength to maintain your boundaries. This I would call *A Sibling Response Normal.*

Normal is an objective concept and short of a physical psychiatric disorder, an oxymoron by definition: we each have our own concept of what normal is. One person might eat lobster tails for breakfast and another might consider that not normal—you should only have breakfast food for your first meal of the day. "Normal" is based on what we are taught as we grow up and we live with this. Perhaps it's why there are so many unhappy families. People from two different backgrounds suddenly come together and are supposed to accept each other's way of thinking. Back in the old days, we just accepted our plight, but now we realize that we no longer have to. The flexibility that once made marriages work is no longer there. We are two normal people who have two different concepts of normalcy and we are expected to live together as though we think alike. The trick to blending and accepting the concept of normalcy is compromise. Without compromise there could be no happiness in the family structure.

Repressed anger is often due to the fact that a sibling recognizes an intolerable situation that others in the family are accepting. They often feel that they would be condemned if they spoke out against the addicted member of the family. The truth is that expressing one's anger regarding the situation is healthy. Keeping resentment inside you leads to more frustration and anger. These emotions fester if they are not released and can eventually lead to a breakup within the family. One meeting room that I went to had a saying on the board that aptly summed up these repressed feelings: *Holding onto resentment is like drinking poison and waiting for the other person to die.*

Your addicted family member has their concept of normal, too. I call this *Addicted Normal.* When this disease first hits, one hopes for a quick resolution and that their loved one will be quickly back in the fold, living their concept of normal. Unfortunately, their concept of normal (at one time an offshoot of their parents') *has now changed* due to an altered production of the chemicals in the brain. Their normal now is to get high and this will never change. It can be treated and this is the goal of both Detox and Rehab. However, as we've discussed, treatment is not a cure. There is no cure. The addict must work conscientiously on a daily (sometimes hourly) basis to fight their forever-normal attraction to getting high. This becomes their way of life and when and if they decide to stay straight it is a constant fight to remain in recovery. I once heard an addict, many years sober, state that every day that he awakened his fight to stay sober began again. Only by going to meetings (NA or AA) and working his program could he continue his fight to stay sober and aware of how devastating life would be should he relapse.

This may sound discouraging, but as I previously mentioned, this is an insidious disease that has the potential to destroy whatever normalcy a family may have. The hope is, when or if the addict hits their bottom and decides to go for help, that they stay with their program. My daughter has gone through four rounds of Rehab and Detox. After the first round she claims to have had four months of clean time; I doubt that she had even two months. She just recently called me to boast that she got her two-month-clean tag from NA. This is a start. It makes me as proud as when she made the honor roll or graduated from college cum laude. You can now see how our concept of normal can change while theirs cannot. I have altered my way of thinking to accept any positive change while she is still in a constant fight to not give in to the ever-present pull of the drugs.

One of the most shocking enlightenments that I had with this disease was about the concept of love. Z was always a happy child with a great sense of humor who loved life and her family. Her sense of humor and happiness seem to have dwindled as the disease has progressed. This is one of the concepts that therapy can help us deal with. What appears to be is not always what is. When she is in recovery she loves us very much. At this time she is Dr. Jekyll. When she relapses, all the good feelings that we have felt while she was in recovery disappear as she morphs into Mr. Hyde. Living with an addict in the family has certainly helped me to understand this story: Dr. Jekyll was addicted to laudanum (an opiate). He then became Mr. Hyde to keep himself supplied with this intoxicant. As Mr. Hyde, he brought hard times upon himself and those who knew him.

While the addict is getting high, the only love that they have is for the drugs. Keep in mind that this is not your family member, it's the addict. My daughter high is not my daughter straight. They are two different people with two different mindsets. The straight daughter is remorseful for having wronged us. She hates herself for the pain that she has caused to the family and sincerely means what she says. She would do anything at this time to have never used drugs and to never again use drugs. This is the family member that we remember and loved as a child.

For some, the first trip to the recovery center is the winner. According to The National Institute on Drug Abuse the relapse rate for substance disorder is between 40% and 60%. This, however, includes those who are on methadone and Suboxone maintenance. This does not tell the real truth though it may sound a bit better than the actual figure for those that are in actual recovery. The person that chooses to enter into a maintenance program is not technically considered to be in recovery since they are still using a substance capable of producing a euphoric effect. Does this mean that your loved one should not enter into a maintenance program? Not at all. These programs have their place. They are used to the patient that suffers from habitual relapse and has suffered overdoses as a result. Weighing to pros against the cons it is always better to stand on the side of saving a life versus standing on principal and seeing a loved one die. After speaking with a friend with long term sobriety he summed it up as "No, it may not be perfect sobriety but something is better than nothing especially if the potential is to save a life. For those who are in actual recovery, the rate of relapse is 90%, so obviously there are some addicts that do remain sober after their first attempt at rehabilitation. We should never give up hope. I think it is in our nature to hope and the disappointment that results when a relapse occurs is what creates the compassion fatigue, which I feel is a euphemism for throwing in the towel or giving up. One in every ten succeeds, and we can always hope our loved one is that one.

Perhaps compassion fatigue comes from trying to avoid the guilt that we feel for allowing this disease to affect our family. Can we ever do that? I know that many times I felt as though I just wanted *to stop worrying* when my daughter relapsed. No matter how many meetings you go to on how to live a normal existence, you don't ever stop worrying not to mention the severe aggravation that accompanies this worry. No matter how well you may be versed in the intricacies of the disease, we all make the mistake of trying to converse rationally with our loved one when they are in active addiction, while they are in a totally irrational state. This adds to the resultant compassion fatigue. As a family member, I personally believe that worry and aggravation are our part of this disease and that at meetings we try to learn how to manage this worry but it never leaves us.

Sliding Along The Slippery Slope

After moving out of the house, Z somehow managed to land an excellent job at an upscale restaurant. She started out as a line chef and was promised the opportunity for advancement if she practiced her craft well. The benefits were excellent and she truly seemed happy. She claimed to be straight, a statement which I had heard on numerous occasions and didn't believe. Oh how I wish that I could have believed, but past experience had taught me to wait and see what developed.

I had always bragged about her successes at her past employments to the people I knew. Now she was starting yet another new job. At first, as was her pattern, she excelled. She received compliments and eventually there was a promise of a promotion as soon as a position opened. This too was a part of her pattern. Although skeptical, as always, I was proud. Always the optimist, I was also seeing an improvement in the way she spoke and looked. I wouldn't bet the farm on it, but she actually did seem to be straight. For the life of me I can't understand what triggers her but it seems that as soon as she gets to the point where she starts to excel at her job, she begins her decline. I guess this is the path of the self-destructive personality.

A self-destructive personality is something that an achiever cannot understand. The person who has the type of personality that drives them to success works hard to achieve and constantly thinks in a positive way that directs them towards their goals. Then there is the under achiever who feels that upward mobility is a good goal but that reaching the top is not something that is within their potential. The person with a self-destructive personality is the saddest of people. They know that they have the potential to obtain success, but as soon as it is within their grasp they do something to reverse their path. I believe that the majority of addicts feel at home being this type of person. I know my daughter does, and she is in no way unique to this group.

After losing a job she cleans house, gets sober, and sets out to find another restaurant to work in. She does not just look for any job, but rather seeks out a place that offers advancement plus benefits—definite positive steps toward success. When she finds such a place she stays clean for a period of time and her talents are usually recognized. She comes home with compliments and both my wife and I have moments of happiness, waiting for the promotion that will perhaps build up her self-esteem and help her to continue along her journey of recovery. Once she reaches a certain point, we suddenly begin to hear the familiar story about someone at work harassing her, or for no reason they hired another chef and the position she was waiting for was given to another.

This usually coincides with Z slurring her words and me finding her half on the bed and half on the floor, asleep. Perhaps as family members who fall into this trap we fit into the definition of insanity. After all, we watch the same scenario time after time, expecting a different result. This feeling is usually left to the parental segment of the family as other family members are more apt to relinquish their bonds sooner than a mother or father.

Well, it seemed that this job was no different. While sober, she decided to move back into our house. She knew that Beau had to find his own place to stay—after the last bout he was not welcome. After working for several months and doing well, the down phase of the cycle emerged. A new chef was hired and he was harassing her. She suddenly went from loving her job to wanting to become a server. She was written up by the new chef for having to go to the bathroom. Everything she was saying would have made sense, in her defense, if this were the first time that this was occurring.

This was, sadly, not the first time, and I could only wait and see what would occur but I knew that I would not like it. The sick feeling was slowly returning to both my wife and me.

Z is now in her thirties—an adult. The fact that she still has not attained adult status is both her fault and ours—her parents. At this point in her life, she was supposed to be capable of making decisions and living on her own. Due to our overprotective nature and her addictive personality, she either didn't care to, or was not capable of, figuring out how to deal with the repercussions of her negative actions.

When parents are overprotective of their children, it reduces their ability to develop fundamental adult decision-making skills and therefore they remain childlike, never progressing toward understanding the consequences of decisions—whether right or wrong. That is one of the reasons that Al-Anon is important for the family members, especially the mother and father of the addict. Organizations such as Al-Anon and Nar-Anon can help you cope with thoughts, answer questions, and help you to keep your sanity when you need help. You might be thinking, how can I allow my child to live in such conditions? How can I not give my child money if they need it? (And how do I fight the urge to do so?) I didn't raise them to live like this. What did I do wrong to make them turn out like this? These are all questions that I have heard others ask many times and have often asked them myself.

What tends to keep one from going to fellowship meetings is shame. The shame is on you for not going. At these meetings you will meet people who suffer with the same problems that you suffer from. I have brought this up before and will continue to throughout this book because of the importance of these organizations in *helping the family member become familiar with and live with* this disease.

So back to Z: my daughter now had this great job and the same bull was starting again. I was preparing for a relapse. My wife was telling me to stop being so negative. My daughter once accused me of treating the clients at the meetings that I attend differently than I treated her. I asked what she meant by this and she said that when they relapsed and returned to treatment I would give them encouragement and say that relapse was part of the disease and I was proud that they had made the choice to return to treatment. Relapse may be considered part of the disease but should not be considered a part of the recovery process. Returning to treatment after a relapse is a traumatic experience for the person suffering from the disease of addiction. This is especially true for the "Newbie" (one who is new to the treatment process) who feels that much more shame for having relapsed after their first treatment and has to return and face those that treated them in the past, as well as those they have bonded with while in treatment. Returning to treatment is a major step for those that have been in recovery and relapsed, regardless of the amount of time they were out in the world but for the addict new to the disease, relapse is a new situation that they may not yet realize is common and they should be proud of their decision to return to treatment. You should encourage your loved one and explain to them that with very few exceptions, most addicts have relapsed and will and should be welcomed back. Encouraging them to succeed is also part of the support process. Again, if you find yourself on the wrong side of rational in your discussion with your loved one, step back, get someone else to speak with them, and remember, speaking rationally to your loved one is not always an easy accomplishment.

I asked myself if Z was right. I felt bad but thought through what she had said before I responded. I organized my thoughts instead of reacting instinctively and saying something that I would have to apologize for later. I realized that the situations were different. The difference was that one client *realized that they needed help* to once again regain control of their life, whereas Z always claimed that she had not relapsed, thus continuing along the path of denial, self-destruction, and active addiction. This was a difference that could be the determining factor between life and death as well as a perfect example of the manipulative capabilities of the addict.

Here she was, trying to use the idea of someone's admitting a relapse and going for help to try to make me feel guilty for urging her to seek help; meanwhile she was getting high and claiming that she had not relapsed. Though I realized that I was being played, remarkably I kept my composure. Another factor to keep in mind is that you cannot act objectively when dealing with a family member, especially when you know that they are trying to manipulate you. You should never be able to find a therapist who would treat their own family. The lawyer that defends himself has a fool for a client.

Going for help is an act for which you cannot be fired. Addiction is covered under the American with Disabilities Act and is therefore treated as an illness. If Z had followed the proper methods of notification and had gone into treatment, she would most likely still have had her job. Instead, she opted for the path of blaming others for her problems and eventually got fired. Again, Z's behavior pattern is not unique in the world of addiction. Again, she was incomeless (as was Beau) and her bills were once again coming due. So again, she was on the prowl for a job. By this time, jobs were becoming harder for her to find. She had already worn out her welcome in many local restaurants. Kitchen work is hard and the restaurateur needs dependable staff. This clearly omits the chef with a known addiction problem. She went out daily but could not find a job. She was genuinely discouraged.

She would hug her mother (who was giving her moral support) and scowl at me (who was telling her she'd lose the next job anyway if she didn't get straight first). The fact is, you cannot maintain a job while in active addiction and with few exceptions, you cannot get straight on your own. Slowly, her situation deteriorated again until she reached the point where her addiction was too obvious to hide. Due to the progressive nature of addiction, the patient will eventually get to the point where they will lose control of their concept of right and wrong. They will wind up doing things that you do not want to hear about to get their drugs. Their human survival instincts become honed towards obtaining drugs to prevent the withdrawal effects. This can manifest in changing one's instinct to eat, sleep, and work into the instinct to procure drugs at all cost—legal or not. Hunger for food is replaced by the hunger to use their drug of choice, thus we see our loved one losing weight, becoming unkempt, and eventually living on the street.

One day, Z told my wife she had made an appointment with a doctor that specialized in the treatment of addiction. I am very skeptical of these doctors. Yes, there are some that are dedicated to working with the addict to help bring them down to a functional level, but you must be very selective about whom you choose. Most are in the practice of *substituting one addiction for another*. Yes, they will get you off of heroin, but they will substitute it with Suboxone or Subutex. Suboxone contains buprenorphine (an opioid medication used to prevent withdrawal) plus naloxone (referred to as a blocker) that has the ability to block the intoxicating effects. Suboxone allows the heroin addict to function somewhat normally. Subutex, on the other hand, is only buprenorphine and should be considered less useful when used as a substitute for opioid addiction. Both Suboxone and Subutex have great benefit in the detox process, helping the addict come off of the opiates in a civil manner (known as a soft landing), by avoiding many of the illnesses associated with withdrawal. When given as a substitute for the opiate, the client soon becomes addicted to the buprenorphine. This drug can be harder to kick than heroin. To get off of drugs, one must make the decision to do just that. It will take approximately two weeks, plus one week to become drug free, and another week to begin to function in a manner that allows them to begin therapy. The process of detoxification lasts considerably longer than the allotted time that the insurance companies allow for.

The use of Sebutex and Suboxone is beginning to gain acceptance among addiction professionals. Although to be in recovery one must be in a state of abstinence, with the amount of death due to overdoses climbing daily, the use of Sebutex and Suboxone has become an acceptable alternative to death. Ultimately, they should be reserved for chronic relapsers. As they say, "something is better than nothing." I would rather have a live child than a dead one who tried to do it right and failed.

Z found a good doctor—she was lucky. He was going to put her on Suboxone and reduce the dose until she was clean. This is what she told me and with the confidentiality laws (HIPPA) I would have to accept her at her word. She was an adult and her doctor was not permitted to speak to me without her permission.

She seemed to be doing well. The feeling of relief is measurable when your child speaks coherently without slurring their words. You learn to look for the positive signs and to take what comes. It was at this time that Beau seemed to want to get straight, too. I accepted this as a major step forward. I don't know what triggered this feeling in him but you don't ask why one decides to take a path toward sobriety; perhaps it was his family telling him that he would be more accepted if he was in recovery…or maybe they just threatened to cut off his support. Perhaps what triggered this sudden urge to get straight was the fact that he truly seemed to be in love with my daughter, and we refused to accept him when he was using (thus preventing Z from getting straight) and not employed.

His family up north had insurance coverage for him and he was able to enter into a paid Detox and a treatment program at a good facility. An addict, especially one who is new to recovery, cannot remain sober if they are hanging around someone who is in active addiction—eventually they will relapse. It is for this reason that a facility will give a client, should they relapse, the option of returning to Detox and starting treatment over, or vacating the facility. Whether it was his parent's advice or his own idea, his willingness to enter into treatment was a positive step and should be applauded.

After several relapses you will probably be tired of hearing the same story again and again. "This time" may also be another failed attempt. Once again, you may feel let down and perhaps like you've been played for the fool. Please don't feel this way. One never knows which trip to Rehab will be the *successful* one. Yes, you are probably thinking, "How many times do I have to go through this? How many times do I have to get my hopes up just to be let down again?" To be truthful, no one can answer that question. As many times as it takes is the best answer I can give. If your loved one lives long enough, they will eventually feel that click and enter into long-term sobriety.

My feeling about Beau was that if he got straight, perhaps Z would try to get straight also. She claimed to love Beau very much. I was curious to see whether this love would be strong enough to keep them on the road to recovery. I am also quite sure that Beau's parents had the same feelings about my daughter. Anyway, Beau took the proper steps. He started by getting the drugs out of his system by entering into Detox and then went to Rehab where he underwent intensive therapy. The rehabilitation process usually takes thirty days to complete but he was in for longer. Most people need more than thirty days for the metamorphosis from the addict with the cravings for their particular drugs to a sober person who has the self-esteem and fortitude to resist relapsing. So this looked like a positive sign. From Rehab, Beau went into a sober-living facility where he could be in a structured environment while learning how to live a normal life and seek employment. Low and behold, shock of all shocks, his structured residence was for *men only*. It did have a separate residence for women but not in the vicinity of the men's facility. I mention this to stress the point that while in active addiction one cannot trust what your loved one says: legitimate facilities segregate by sex.

His rehabilitation took approximately three months. He came out a more confident (and sober) person. Z was still using Suboxone and for a while was able to function, but eventually returned to using heroin. There she was, using heroin and waiting for her true love to leave treatment so that she could lure him back into using. This drug is like scabies: it just does not go away unless treated properly. Without a job, she had no insurance and without insurance, she would have to go to a county facility, which she refused to do.

The Broward Addiction Recovery Center (known as BARC) is a well-run system of treatment, more than adequate to prepare the addict to meet the future if they are serious about getting straight. As I may have previously stated, I may have spoiled my children a bit, and Z felt BARC was below her. We could not force her into treatment. The bottom line is other than Marchman Acting someone you cannot force them into treatment once they have reached the legal age.

And so, Z overdosed again. Because she happened to know the pusher, (Z makes friends easily) he called Beau, who then called the paramedics, who got there in time to revive her. I truly thank him for this as the common response is to turn the other way. The most amazing thing about this is that when she told us the story she seemed *proud* that she had overdosed and survived. How broken her thinking process had become.

Perhaps it was a second brush with death, or Beau threatening to break up with her if she didn't get straight, that made her sit us down. She said that she had gone back to the addiction doctor and he had prescribed Suboxone again and told her how to taper off of it to become drug free. Of course, I had my doubts about her success, but it was so good to hear that she wanted to get straight again.

I've learned not to ask questions about my daughter's willingness to get straight. The thought of it alone was enough to trigger a positive response in me. She said that the doctor was getting her off the drugs and that she wanted to go up north with Beau to a very strict halfway house that she had heard about located somewhere in Pennsylvania. I felt positive about this for several reasons. First of all, she would be on her own. This would be a first and perhaps it would help her to mature. Second of all, it was one of the few positive steps that I had seen her take in a long time and when your loved one is chronically relapsing, one learns to accept whatever positive situation comes along.

My wife was somewhat ambiguous in her feelings. On the one hand, she knew that Z was old enough to go out on her own, and that a move up north could be a good thing. On the other hand, she also knew that she would miss her terribly. (File that under *codependency*.) As previously stated, what would otherwise be considered a normal parental reaction to a situation, can be construed to be codependency so you should not feel guilty if you think you are trying to help your family member and suddenly find that what you are doing is negative.

Suppose you have a child who is a doctor and wants to open an office. He asks if you could lend him some money so that he doesn't have to pay the high interest rates that the bank charges. He says he will sign a note guaranteeing that he will repay you. You agree. That would be considered helping your child get a start in life. Now, let's suppose you have another child who is a drug abuser. He comes to you high as a kite and asks you to lend him $20 to buy clothes. To do so would be enabling. Why? Because there is a certainty that your doctor son is going to open an office. Your addicted-to-heroin son is more likely to go naked than to not use the cash to buy heroin. If you think this sounds cruel, think of this: he buys a bag of heroin, overdoses, and dies. Does it sound cruel not to give him the money now?

We were now faced with a new situation. One that perhaps you too can identify with: how should we feel when our family member announces that they are suddenly going to leave the nest? If she was really going up north to start a new and sober life, great. But first, Z was going to New Jersey where she and Beau would live with his mother. Then, when there was an opening at the Pennsylvania facility, they would move into separate living facilities. To me this sounded too good to be true. As fate would have it, it was. Apparently, on a previous trip to the north, they had gotten into trouble with the law and she had been too afraid to tell us about it. This was why she and Beau moved up north and in with his mother: so they could go to court where they were given a reprimand. They got off easy and as of this time they are still doing well.

Z just received her ninety-day medallion and has a new sponsor. These are words that I never thought I would be able to write. Do I, by any stretch of the imagination, think that she is finally on the road to recovery? In no way am I kidding myself into believing that the nightmare is over. Yes, I am a little more optimistic today than yesterday, and tomorrow I will be another day more optimistic than today, but I will always have the fear of relapse hanging over me. Update: It turned out that Z was counting the days she was on Suboxone maintenance as recovery time, which in reality it is not. She was in New Jersey then, and I was in Florida. Sadly, she did not deserve that ninety-day medallion.

Still More to Learn About the Disease

The first thing that you must understand about this disease is that there is no end to it. Although addicts can enter into a phase of remission, there is no cure for the disease of addiction. No one knows what will trigger a relapse or why. Other than some type of chemical release in the brain, there doesn't seem to be a reason for many years of sober living suddenly being at risk of going down the tubes. AA and NA or whatever fellowship programs your loved one may choose are absolutely necessary. So often a relapse can be prevented by the addict simply going to a meeting, speaking out, and seeking help. They can call their support group or sponsor who will be there for them. Should the sponsor be unavailable when a situation arises, the person suffering from this disease should have a support group available so that they are never left to their own resources to cope with a sudden urge to use. *Unless the addict attends meetings and gets support and a sponsor, there most likely will be a relapse.*

I often compare the program that an addict works to the chemotherapy that a cancer patient must go through to get the cancer into remission. Both diseases are equally deadly. Yes, perhaps this disease did start out by choice. That, however, is in the past and at this point your loved one suffers from a disease that, if they do not work a program, see a therapist, and get support from their loved ones, they will have a much greater chance of relapse which can lead to their death. If we put aside the negative connotation that the populace attaches to this disease and think in a rational manner, we can come to the conclusion that most people die from diseases of choice.

Is addiction a disease of choice? I believe it may start out that way because, especially at this time with all the knowledge out there, we know that a drug such as pot can be addicting. One can therefore, assume that the use of a substance causing intoxication has *the potential* for addiction. If you choose to use this as a way to socialize that is your choice. Does everyone who smokes pot become addicted? No, but let us agree that the potential is there. As those drugs (such as pot) that are not physically addicting are psychologically addicting, pot addiction would be a disease of choice. Compare this to a disease such as brain cancer or stomach cancer which you have no control over: *not* a disease of choice for the purpose of comparison.

However, *once you enter into active addiction the choice is gone*. At this time you need help to enter into a remission. Once in a remission you are once again in a position of becoming a victim of a disease of choice. Even if there are strong urges, you must fight that pull to the brink of using: the choice to pick up is ultimately yours to make.

The influence of family support in the recovery process cannot be overstated. Let's review the phases an addict goes through when he or she decides to enter into treatment. The first is detoxification. The breaking of the actual physical addiction can take as little as three days or go on for a week or two. Sometimes in severe cases it can take several weeks for the addict to fully shake the residual effects that the drugs have upon them. At this time the addict is very emotional and their thoughts are self-focused rather than about what they have done to their family. Until they are totally drug free and feeling right, you cannot expect them to be repentant or considerate of how you feel. They have just been through a very tough time and probably still have ill feelings. Be patient, this will not last long unless there were extenuating circumstances.

Soon after Detox they will usually begin to miss their family and feel extremely regretful for the pain that they have caused.

The detoxification process is meant to get your loved one off the drugs that they have used for a period of time and you may not have been aware of how many drugs they were using. Although the time it takes to get to where they don't get dope sick any more may be relatively short, the time it takes for them to begin to think in a more rational capacity will certainly be longer. Your loved one may have been using for many years. Perhaps even for several years before you became aware of their situation. Suddenly, they are put into a facility that is charged with the almost-impossible task of getting them up on their feet and acting rational in a week's time. The Detox centers are, for the most part, fairly successful with the control of withdrawal syndrome. When you visit your loved one in Detox, be prepared for negative feedback and perhaps outbursts. This may not be easy for you to accept, but be patient and give them time and you will see a change. Keep in mind that they do love you and at this time it is still the disease that is doing the speaking. This is a hard concept to grasp and harder to accept, especially for a parent. You spend your life devoted to your child, try to do what is best for them (which usually sneaks into the range of enabling when it involves an addict), and now here you sit, listening to them berate you and blame you for all that has happened to them. Please don't feel that I am scolding you if you do enable your loved one. The line between helping and enabling is so fine that you don't even realize when you have crossed it. I have mentioned this many times so that you will try *to think about what you are about to do before you do it.* Remember, hindsight is 20/20. So don't beat yourself up if a therapist tells you that you have enabled your love one. Instead, use it as a learning experience. All I can say is that the following week, if you return to the support meeting (Family Night) you will see a more normal response to your input. This usually continues and you'll see weekly improvement until one week, you suddenly notice that the person you know and love is "back."

It is around this time that shame and low self-esteem begin to consume the patient. Therefore, it is also around this time that a loving family can be an extremely important factor in the recovery process. Now is the time for the family to express to the addict how proud they are that they have taken the positive steps toward sobriety. This is also the time for the family to express to the addict that what they have done in the past *shall remain in the past* as long as the addict chooses to continue to work positively in their recovery process. This is going to be a long and cumbersome fight for all of your family that will never end. They are going to require your support. They will need you to help build their self-esteem and to help them overcome their guilt for the actions that they have previously committed, causing them great shame. It will be hard to remember that the person that was in active addiction is not the same as the one who is now desperately seeking help and fighting to stay sober. The hardest part for family members at this time is to accept this as a disease and to help in the fight. Every instinct that we have built up inside of ourselves is yelling to us that *they have no disease! They are committing a criminal act by using for the sole purpose of attaining a euphoric state.*

Taking the time to read up on this disease will help you to understand what is happening. They must never forget that they are just one use away from relapse—nor should you. If they are in a program, over time they will begin to develop a routine that will make it easier to live sober and work. As time passes, maintaining sobriety will eventually become a way of life for the addict with a long-term recovery plan. The life of the addict at this time is in turmoil and often their family cannot understand why.

It's because they have just come from a non-functional way of life where their only thought was how to get their next fix. They suddenly entered into a controlled environment with eight to ten hours per day of constant therapy then—boom—are released back "into the world" and the family often thinks that all is well and *why can't they function like they did before they entered into the disease?* Unfortunately, it doesn't work that way. The fact is, even if your loved one is one of the few that never relapses, their thought process has been altered and they will *need a life of support*, be it their program, therapy, or a combination of both. They will progress towards a more acceptable lifestyle as time goes on, but the most important fact to keep in mind (and I am repeating it for a reason) is that once they have *crossed the line into the world of addiction, there is no cure.*

Upon completion of the treatment phase of the program, the client may return to their prior residence or (hopefully) enter into a halfway residence. Regardless of what the insurance industry supports, entering into a sober-living residence, often referred to as a halfway house, is a significant part of recovery. Unfortunately, they are not covered by insurance. Perhaps this is not as bad as it may sound as this is the point in treatment where the client is supposed to develop a routine that will aid them in their growth into recovery. For the first time in the recovery process the client is somewhat on their own, although they are still living in a structured environment. It is here that they must seek employment, pay bills, and cook and clean for themselves. They are strongly encouraged to attend meetings and also are randomly drug tested to check on their sobriety.

The First Phase of Treatment: Detox

Detox is the first step of your loved one's journey to sobriety. This is where they are sent to withdraw from the drugs (this includes alcohol) in a safe environment, supervised by a medical specialist in the field. This can be compared to basic training as your loved one is not going to feel well for a while. At this stage, they will have thoughts of leaving treatment as, even though they are given medications to help them come down gently, they still undergo the ill feelings of withdrawal. The doctor or his nurse practitioner meet with the new patient (client) and complete an intake examination, similar to the admission procedure in a hospital. Upon determining what the client's addictions are and any illnesses that they might have (such as Hepatitis or HIV), the nurse practitioner and the doctor then determine a course of treatment that generally takes about a week—hopefully with as few side effects as possible.

Detox can be thought of as the physical portion of treatment. Technical information is taken such as name, date of birth, address, emergency contact, insurance information, and DOCs (as well as non-DOCs). They have to pee in a cup, usually under the supervision of a technician, and a drug test is performed by placing a small tablet into the cup with approximately twelve dip sticks attached to it, each with a different reagent that tests for a different type of drug. After a few minutes these reagent sticks are compared to a color chart, usually located on the cup, and the results are determined. The medical staff have now determined what drugs that the client (your beloved addict) has in their system. The intake professional will then try to ascertain if there are any additional illnesses or medical conditions so that arrangements can be made for medications/treatments to be provided.

Upon completion of the necessary paperwork, the patient is introduced to the nursing and medical staff and shown to their room where they will live for the next week or so. Their file is then reviewed by the medical staff and a program of treatment is initiated that will aid your loved one as they physically withdraw from the drugs that they are addicted to. The primary purpose of detoxification is to help the addict withdraw safely and with as few scars as possible. This is a point that some professionals leave open for debate, feeling that too soft of a landing may reduce an addict's fear of a relapse. I can see both sides of this argument: yes, it may reduce the fear of relapse, but it also may increase the fear of re-entering into Detox should another relapse occur if the addict is too sick from withdrawal.

If the facility is reputable, at the end of a week or so your loved one should be almost through the detoxification process. Please don't expect this to be a perfect process. Your loved one has likely been using for a long time, probably a lot longer than they have admitted to you, and you shouldn't expect that in a seven-to-ten day period their system will be completely detoxified.

Although this portion of treatment is devoted to detoxification (the physical portion of treatment), most Detox centers also have therapists on staff. The addict may begin counseling at this stage when and if they feel well enough to attend the sessions. AA, NA, or any other program is also available for the addict. Often the residents can attend meetings on the premises or if they are well enough, the facility may bus them to a meeting. The food is often described as better than average (if they are in a private facility). For most addicts this may be the first time they've slept in a clean bed or eaten nutritious food in a long time. Surprisingly, aside from the rotten feeling of withdrawal (and the feelings of guilt and shame beginning to sneak into their thoughts), this is usually a positive experience for the addict.

This is also the place of panic for the first-timer and their family. The addict enters into the unknown, sometimes it's even the first time away from home, and they are suddenly cast into this new scenario of shame, guilt, and fear (and of friends and family finding out about their disease). There is a void that opens up as they are in a situation that they have never before experienced. They are in fear of the beginning of an agonizing detoxification process which they have no factual knowledge of other than what they have been told by their acquaintances. For the family, the same is about to happen. Their loved one has just left them looking scared, sick, and high, they know nothing of what lies ahead for them, and in their subconscious perhaps they feel they don't require this treatment as they are *not really an addict*. The fact that the addict often cannot contact the family for days adds to the fear of the unknown.

Detox centers are there to help and do as fine a job as can be expected with the time allotted by the insurance companies. They are usually given a week to render the addict drug free: this could be someone who has been using many different drugs for several years and the removal of some of these have the potential to cause death during the detox process. They are also expected to have them ready to face six to eight hours a day with a therapist who will try to rearrange their thinking process.

Your loved one is now safer than they've been for the first time in (insert however long they have been using). You should use this time to relax if possible, for in a week they will enter into the rehabilitation portion of treatment (assuming that they don't suddenly up and leave Detox). If the treatment center has a Family Night meeting, you will be asked to interact with your loved one and the group at that time.

The inpatient Detox center functions much the same as a hospital. The patient's vital signs, blood pressure, and heart rate are monitored to make sure that they have not experienced any health problems during their withdrawal. Gradually, the amount of drugs the patient is using to aid in the withdrawal process is tapered down until the regimen can be stopped. The patient may then be placed on antidepressants and tranquilizers (not in the benzodiazepine family), as at this time anxiety is the norm. They may also still be experiencing signs of withdrawal such as tremors, anxiety, belligerence, and sometimes seizures.

As this epidemic spreads, the treatment in government facilities is becoming better. If you don't have insurance for your loved one, do not feel that all is lost. Do a little research to find out which facilities around you are better than others. There are some that offer a soft landing (they aid the patient with medication as they taper off the drugs that they are addicted to). Then there are those that monitor the patient to make sure that they do not have a life-threatening condition but offer nothing to ease the detoxification process other than a trip to the emergency room should the patient need it. Do your research and try to get your loved one into one of the better facilities. There are also private treatment centers that offer scholarships to those that are needy. Google some of the centers and ask questions such as: what are their certifications? Are they accredited locally? Statewide? Are there any complains against them (call the state)?

Back to the topic of Detox, clients are fed well and as mentioned, sometimes these are the first good meals that they have had in a very long time (if they are lucky to feel well enough to eat). Sleeping quarters are clean and therapy may or may not begin here. There are also daily Alcoholic Anonymous or Narcotics Anonymous meetings for those that feel well enough to attend. It is at Detox that the addict makes their first acquaintance with other addicts who are trying to get sober. It is here that they begin to form bonds. They may meet an addict who is returning to the same treatment center where they are to go after Detox. Your first thought as a parent may be, "I don't want my family member associating with other addicts!" Remember: your *family member is an addict*. This statement may cause you to react adversely as there is always that feeling of denial where your loved one is concerned and you have just found out that they suffer from this disease for the first time. Now however, is the time for them to support each other along the road to recovery. They attend meetings together and speak to each other as only addicts knows how to. So let the professionals handle the different processes and go to meetings and learn. An educated family member is so important along this journey.

When the patient is technically considered detoxified they are then sent to the treatment center to begin the process of rehabilitation. Very seldom does a patient come out of Detox fully ready for Rehab. It usually takes another few days (or weeks) before the patient feels well enough to really function. It is not uncommon for the patient to suffer seizures or to act as if they are still detoxing. By the second week, however, the change in their behavior is noticeable, and phase two of the treatment process can begin in earnest.

The Treatment Center

At Rehab, as the treatment center is also referred to, your loved one is assumed to be drug free. This is true to a certain extent. However, there always seems to be some residual withdrawal that may last for days/weeks. They are free from drugs that have the *potential to cause relapse or any type of high* but they might be on drugs to control anxiety, treat depression or certain psychiatric disorders, or any required to treat medical conditions such as hypertension. Keep in mind that although this disease may have affected your child or family member, it knows no distinction as to age, race, sex, or creed. It is perhaps the only equal-opportunity effector around.

The addictive behavior may last for awhile so don't be surprised if your loved one acts nasty or gruff when you first see them. They still love you and as things progress you will see a change in their behavior. There also may be some prevailing physical symptoms that pop up during the very early stages of treatment such as the seizures or aggressive outbursts I mentioned before. So don't be offended if you say something that triggers an irrationally aggressive response. It is not necessarily what you said that triggered this response but the fact that they are still in the process of ridding their body of the toxins that they have accumulated over time. You and most family members may hope and believe that after Detox your loved one will behave normally, but this only happens in the fictitious *Health Insurance Book of Rules and Regulations*.

Rehab is where the addict or alcoholic, if you prefer to treat the two as separate entities, begins the actual therapeutic steps toward recovery. Now that the first step of getting drug free is complete, intensive therapy can begin as the second step. In some places this occurs for just the addict; others have a plan to bring the family members into this healing process. "Healing" isn't a good term as it might suggest that the addict can be cured (or "healed"). *There is no cure for this disease.* Please do not get your hopes up as I did, and as so many others have, who welcomed their members home after their first treatment, thinking that they left the hospital cured. This disease will be a continual struggle that the addict fights for the rest of their lives and relapse often is a part of this process. This fight does get easier as the addict's clean time progresses. Eventually, the program that they choose to work (along with therapy if they choose it) becomes a way of life. The addict fits these daily meetings and fellowshipping events into their routine, and the stress of the commitment to these daily events begins to diminish.

So, Rehab is the second step in the recovery process. It is where the addict begins to receive intensive therapy. This is the part of treatment where the therapist will somehow have to break through the armor that a lot addicts and their families wear, maintaining that they "do not need treatment," and they are "not addicts, they just like to get high." This is likely the toughest part of the job for the therapist. Often there is a reluctance on the part of the parent or family member to accept the fact that their loved one is an addict. This can be understandable initially as there is such a bad connotation associated with the term "addict." For the most part, this reluctance to accept is overcome as the loved one gains more knowledge of the disease. Then the therapy can become effective—if the addict does not take treatment seriously or cannot admit that they need it, there can be no help. The therapist then, must try to pierce the armor that the addict wears so that they can find the underlying issues that led the addict to use, such as abandonment or molestation by a friend or family member, and help them deal with them. This is where meetings that include the family become important. Addressing these matters together is a great help, both as a means to finding root causes and to show support. So often I hear the addict at Family Night speak of the regrets that they have for their actions. So often I hear the family members express these same regrets. Often the addict fears any type of contact with their family because of the abuse they have put them through as they went through the motions of procuring their needed drugs. The addict carries this guilt around and often avoids contact with their loved ones (fearing rejection) thus preventing their therapist from reaching into their emotional past and finding what causes the need to mask their feelings.

At the treatment center (also known as Rehab) the addict is also introduced to the various meeting facilities in the area. They are driven in the transport vans to attend nightly AA or NA meetings, where they can learn the significance of these groups in the mending process as well as the importance of the 12-step program, and how they fit into this mending process. For the point of clarification, not all treatment centers strictly enforce this. Some may require that the clients attend in-house meetings and some may not require that the client attend meetings although most do. There are discussions about other programs that are available such as CoDA (Codependents Anonymous, www.coda.org) or the many faith-based programs such as Celebrate Recovery, a 12-step meeting based on biblical principles and Dharma/Refuge which is based on Buddhist principles. The treatment center will try to expose the clients to as many different meetings as possible but keep in mind that there are a limited number of clients able to attend a particular meeting. Their therapist is tasked with determining whether this particular meeting should be an integrated meeting, or sexually segregated for the client. What may seem insignificant to the untrained family member is very important to the recovery of your loved one. The therapist may determine that it is in the best interest of the client to attend meetings with only members of their own sex. It may be easier for the client to keep their attention on the meeting and the input that is offered if they are not distracted by someone sexually. These fellowship meetings are where the new client learns to make connections with people in recovery that the therapists feel might be helpful for them as they go along their journey toward long-term sobriety.

The addict is also taught to live life in a normal manner in this stage of treatment. They have to follow a schedule, shop, and cook, in addition to attending the meetings and going to therapy. For many this is a totally new experience due to enabling—when the family of the addict feeds, cleans, supplies shelter, and financially supports the addict. How does one know when they are enabling rather than helping? I keep coming back to this question as it is often the crux of the issue in this disease.

The best way to know is by learning about the disease. My rule of thumb is that if *you are not sure you are probably enabling* and this is sure to turn an addict onto the road to relapse. Chances are if you are doing something for your loved one *that they are capable of doing by themselves*, you are enabling. If you are not sure if you should do something for your loved one while they are in treatment, *ask their therapist*. They should be happy to speak with you to help you understand. If the addict has already completed treatment and is in sober living or have their own apartment, then you should allow them to fend for themselves thus *should not be doing anything* for them.

There are those—who have no knowledge of what this disease is truly about—that actually believe that this phase of treatment is a vacation for the addict. I have often heard a family member say that they envy their stay. The addict gets meals, a little recreation on the weekend, and a place to live, so what can be so bad? This phase is actually a very demanding and difficult part of treatment. They are in therapy from early morning until late in the evening. They sit through group sessions where they are picked apart and put back together again on a daily basis. After their daily routine they must attend Family Night meetings or attend program meetings (NA, AA, or whatever program they have decided to enter into). What may seem to be "fun" to the outsider is usually brutal to the addict. So don't be concerned that the insurance company is paying all this money and your loved one went to the beach on Sunday. I can assure you that if they are taking the program seriously this will be a well-deserved trip. On the other hand, if they were not taking the program seriously you would have been notified and they likely would not have been permitted to join the group.

The Halfway House

Time in the halfway house is the part of the rehabilitation process that is often taken the least seriously by those who don't know about addiction or are new to it. This especially goes for the bureaucracies who either don't know or don't care about the significance of this third part of recovery. The person in treatment that is married or must return to work is focused on getting home and returning to normalcy. The young client's thoughts are that they have been cooped up for all this time and once released from rehab they just want to get home to family and friends. These are both hazardous forms of thinking. When the clients leave treatment, they are at their most vulnerable time as far as relapse is concerned. It may sound nice to have them return home and see their old friend, but this is the same situation they left when they were using. There is a very high potential for relapse at this time and although returning home does not guarantee a relapse, it might be best left for a later date.

Like any other potentially terminal disease, the patient and family must take all precautions to prevent a relapse. Although there is this strong desire to return to the outside world there is also an almost universal fear of living in an unsupervised environment or at least, if sobriety is to be maintained successfully, there should be. This occurs due to the fact that the addict knows the potential for relapse (only they can know how strong their urges are). The family member of the first-timer, even if they have some knowledge of this disease, does not comprehend the extent to which the potential for relapse exists. The client, at the time of their completion of rehab, is mixed emotionally, experiencing feelings that were previously masked by their use of drugs. It is hard for them to comprehend that these feelings are normal and legitimate. For the first time in a long time they are experiencing real life and often are not sure how to handle these very real feelings.

I was once at a meeting that illustrates the potential helpfulness of a halfway house: a newly released client suddenly developed strong urges to use. Being new to recovery, she began to panic as her thoughts of using (thus imminent relapse) were almost uncontrollable. She thankfully had the presence of mind to seek out a technician and discuss what was happening. (The technician is someone who works as a kind of overseer whose job it is to keep an eye on the clients. This job requires that they have some expertise in the field of addiction so that they can be of assistance should a situation arise that requires the help of someone with this knowledge.) The Technician explained that this was completely normal and that one of the necessary challenges faced by the client is learning to control these urges. The client has to realize that *there is no cure for this disease and urges and drug dreams are a part of the recovery process.* They must learn to recognize their triggers and try to avoid them. If the client had returned home and the parent was at work at the time that the urges presented, how easily a relapse could have occurred.

The halfway house acts as a bridge between the treatment facility (not real life) and living as a sober person (close to real life but with boundaries). It is a regimented living facility that continues to facilitate the addict's transitions: first from total lack of control, then to totally supervised living, to finally learning how to run their own lives. It is here that they can relate to other addicts experiencing (or who have recently experienced) these feelings and who can help them understand what they are going through.

They are given a clean environment in which to live. They are encouraged to seek employment, attend meetings, work a program of their choice, and get experience with day-to-day life experience. They are given rules and regulations by which they must abide or be faced with penalties which could result in eviction from the facility. They are required or encouraged to attend AA, NA, or meetings of their choice, daily. The clients are encouraged to get a sponsor and gather a support group, two things that they learn how to do while attending meetings and while in treatment. They are required to vacate the premises to seek employment by a certain time each day. The facility holds weekly meetings with mandatory attendance and group discussions are held to ascertain the well-being of the client.

The clients are required clean the facility—part of one day per week is set aside to maintain the cleanliness and livability of their quarters. Although this may seem harsh to the outsider, the intent of the halfway house is to keep the client on a straight line toward living a sober life. These are the disciplines that help to prevent a relapse. There is also random drug testing. Failure here leads to immediate eviction. The client would then be brought back to treatment and the cycle begins again. They can reapply for admission to the halfway facility once treatment is completed and the center has determined that they are once again ready for halfway living.

The usual stay is anywhere from six months to a year. As they progress along their journey toward sobriety they are encouraged to help those that are new to the facility. Bonds are made that sometimes last a lifetime. What they learn there is basically a routine to function in recovery. The addict is with their peers where they develop the necessary skills to maintain their recovery without feeling the stress of having to develop a routine while trying to survive the occurrences of daily living.

IOP: Intensive OutPatient

IOP or Intensive OutPatient therapy also has its place in the recovery process. This is a process that allows the client to continue to receive treatment, usually anywhere from six to thirty hours per week. It is designed to help those who do not or no longer require detoxification from drugs. The client may have completed inpatient treatment or be unable to enter into in-patient treatment. It is a satisfactory method of maintenance of sobriety with intensive therapy and encouragement to attend 12-step meetings. However, as a sole method of treatment, success is not as likely as when combined with inpatient therapy. It can and does work, depending on the addict's willingness to recover. Therapists are less able to monitor (occasionally control) the daily activities of the patient when they are an outpatient. They arrive for therapy but are then on their own recognizance when they leave and only they know if they are doing the right thing. If the client finds that they cannot enter into inpatient treatment, this is a fine alternative. Combined with the determination of someone who wants to work the process and enter into sobriety, it will often be successful.

This is used to a more successful end as a form of therapy for the newly released patient who feels the need for continued therapy but for whatever reason can no longer stay as an inpatient client. They attend a daily therapy session—usually three days per week—at an outpatient facility where their therapist can have contact with their previous therapist and a better outcome becomes a much stronger possibility.

This phase of treatment, when used as an adjunct to inpatient therapy, provides an extra protective barrier against relapse. In the old days, those in recovery felt that attending the program alone (be it NA or AA) was sufficient for those suffering from addiction to recover. As more education concerning this disease became available it became obvious that the use of the drug was a symptom of this disease. *Why the addict felt it necessary to use* was what the disease was really about. Today we know that yes, the abstinence portion of this disease is an important factor in recovery—the physical aspect—but that addressing the psychological aspect of this disease is considered the most important part of the recovery process.

So what does this mean to the addict and their family, trying to decide if IOP is necessary or right for them? That is something that the addict must decide on their own. Forcing them to enter into IOP means that they will be unwilling to cooperate with the therapist. Not willing to go for no reason is not a good sign—and perhaps indicates a greater need for your loved one to attend. The more therapy your loved has, the better their chance for recovery.

My opinion as to whether IOP is a necessary part of the recovery process is—absolutely yes! Most relapses occur early in the recovery process. This is why the reward systems used to encourage those in recovery (key chains, discs or coins/tokens) are *given more frequently during the first year*. Thus, the importance of IOP is almost self-explanatory. Using IOP as an extension of treatment makes good sense, and works.

An experienced addiction therapist can see a relapse coming well before it actually occurs. They have the knowledge to intercede and hopefully prevent it from coming to end-stage. (The actual *act of using the drug* is the end-stage of relapse.) But, the client is in relapse before they actually use. Hopefully the IOP therapist can bring them back before they use.

Yes, going to meetings may also help but truthfully, those attending the meetings are somewhat suspicious of newcomers.

Until they get to know that the Newbie is serious about their recovery, they are hesitant to open up and form a close bond with the new member fresh out of treatment. This is not because they are cliquish. Rather, the rate of relapse with those newly out of treatment is high and *very contagious*. For that reason it takes time for them to get to know the new member and observe and ascertain their seriousness before bonding with them. The exception to this would be the addict who has some clean time and is attending the meeting in an attempt to head off a relapse and share what is happening. Then you will see some of those attending the meeting approach the person to help work them out of their distress.

The Prognosis

The prognosis for this disease may appear to be dismal. This is not true! Yes, there is a very high relapse rate. Does this mean that your family member will not succeed? Absolutely not; there is hope for any addict and I feel that their chances of recovery depend upon how hard they are willing to work, how seriously they take their disease (not in denial), and how much the family is there for support (and not to enable). Eventually, if the addict lives long enough, they will grow tired of living the lifestyle and often enter into a program on their own. The hope for us is that we have managed to survive long enough to see this happen. Once the addict decides that they have had enough and truly wants to enter into sobriety, the success rate improves dramatically. My recommendation is to not follow statistics as they can be deceiving. Each case is an individual one. Your loved one is just one individual who has to decide how much he wants to succeed. Assuming that the family member is now ready to enter into treatment and then recovery, they must be aware of what comes along with the desire to get clean.

Never give up on supporting the addict as long as they keep trying to attain sobriety. Certain circumstances may dictate how you deal with your situation. This does not mean that you don't support your loved one. Let's suppose that you are married to someone that suffers from this disease. They return home late each night totally intoxicated and nasty. They scream, curse, throw thinks, break things, and create a situation that is not conducive for raising children. Does supporting your loved one require you to put your children's welfare in jeopardy? Or course not! Making them leave does not mean you are not supporting them in their attempts toward recovery. You are just looking out for the welfare of the rest of your family and possibly preventing Family Protective Services from removing your children from the house should they be called by someone.

This is a very powerful disease but the power of one's desire to stay clean can and must be stronger. This is likely to be the toughest fight the addict will ever encounter. In one corner there is the champ: Addiction, a disease that has the strength and cunning to break even the bonds of parenthood. Even knowing that they could have their children taken away, the disease still has the power to pull the addict into a relapse. In the other corner is the person who suffers from this disease: our beloved Addict. They have their therapist, their family—who hopefully still shows them love and support—and theirself, who must have a true passion to succeed. To succeed one must be willing to fight hard and work a program of their choice…They must make *recovery* their most *important goal in life*. Once they attend the meetings in their area and the members of the group can see that they are serious about maintaining their sobriety, they will begin to enter into a period of familiarity and acceptance. At this time they form their support group and seek out someone whom they feel compatible with to ask to be their sponsor. Although they are heading in a positive direction, please remember that every day is a new one hence the saying "one day at a time." This is a time of caution for you. Love, support, be proud, but know that at any moment, the police or (even worse) the paramedics could be at your door.

A Deceptive Disease

I speak as both a pharmacist and a parent when I say that addiction is a very deceptive disease. It is most likely genetic in nature and often presents in several family members. This disease is like a compulsive disorder which is identified mostly when the addict acts out in the form of using abusive manifestations: drugs, alcohol, food (eating disorders), sex, or gambling. We see those around us that are compelled to constantly shop, those devoting their whole life to work, putting in eight or ten hour days, or even those watching the television from waking until bedtime. Most people would see no harm in these actions, but people with these compulsions have the potential for more serious addictions. Some of these compulsions may already be a serious problem and have already affected their lifestyle. If an addict's family has compulsive family members, this could account for the lack of belief that their family member could "actually be an addict." Often the therapist's hardest job is convincing not just the addict, but also the family members that they too may suffer from an addiction disorder/compulsion. It is only once these compulsions have been unveiled that treatment may begin. One must realize how hard it is for the therapist to work with the addict when there is negative or no support from the family.

Nothing you might be thinking is a new concept to the therapist. They have seen and heard it all and are trained to function under the handicap of parental denial or compassion fatigue while working to open the minds and eyes of the non-believers. By the way, please do not take what I am saying about family denial personally.

You are not alone and parents who *do believe* that their child is an addict when they first find out about their drug usage *are in the minority*. As previously stated, most family members either believe that this is a phase their loved one is going through—a possible rite of passage—or "just recreational" use. For this reason, I am glad that the insurance companies have begun to expand their twenty-eight day limit. It takes almost that long *just to convince the client and their family member that they have a problem* that requires treatment. It is only after this obstacle is overcome that treatment may begin in earnest.

The person addicted to drugs will put their life in danger, steal from others, destroy relationships, lose jobs, and risk arrest just to fulfill their compulsion to get high. I have seen people lose multi-million-dollar businesses to addiction. Addicted people come from every corner of society and the pervasiveness of this disease has finally opened the minds of families, allowing them to come to the decision to seek help more easily. I see people drive up to the pharmacy in expensive luxury cars, trying to fill quasi-legal prescriptions from pill mills, in states of withdrawal, pleading with the pharmacist to fill their prescriptions.

The disease of addiction is very complicated and is even difficult for addicts to understand. It is a great fight just to educate the addict to the fact that they need help unless something spectacular triggers an event that brings this reality to the surface. Alcoholics may spend a lifetime drinking to excess as this form of addiction is initially acceptable—alcohol is a legal drug. Thus the abuser has an easier time covering up his or her excessive use. They may be the life of the party or reclusive in nature. The quiet ones are the most dangerous to themselves as they are the least likely to be seen as an addict and getting help for them can be difficult.

When I was growing up, I had a neighbor who consumed about a fifth of vodka a day. She was financially well off and had no need to work. She had a quiet personality, so for the most part, few knew that she drank to excess unless she had to ask them to drive her to the liquor store. It was at a time when there were few known addicts and people had little knowledge of addiction so nobody realized that anything was wrong. I remember her husband stating once, "She could drink me under the table. That woman has a wooden leg." It almost sounded as if he was proud that she could drink so much. The problem was that because the alcohol was obtained legally, the excessive use was not frowned upon (as, say, heroin would have been). As long as the alcoholic is able to control their actions and is not exhibiting boisterous, excessive behavior, all is okay. She was able to raise her child, keep a clean house, prepare meals, and provide for her husband. Today, she would be considered a functioning alcoholic. She eventually died of tongue cancer and liver disease—attributed to her excessive drinking.

The infamous pill mills have exacerbated the addiction epidemic epically. Now people can obtain prescriptions for opiates, benzodiazepines, hypnotics (used for sleep), and muscle relaxants (the muscle relaxant was the one that people often used to replace quaaludes when they were taken off the market because of their potential for abuse) by simply walking into a doctor's office. Many offices operate under the cover of being a "Pain Clinic." Patients can walk out with an obscene amount of addictive substances such as oxycodone (30 mg for initial pain relief treatment and then 15 mg used to supplement the effect of the 30 mg), Dilaudid (hydromorphone 2 mg, 4 mg, or 8 mg), or methadone (10 mg also used for breakthrough pain), and Xanax (alprazolam, a benzodiazepine usually 2 mg) which the doctor would claim was used to treat both anxiety due to the pain as well as muscle spasms. Let us not forget that the regimen also includes Soma 350 mg (carisoprodol)—a muscle relaxant having euphoric as well as aphrodisiac properties when taken by itself (see above comment). Taken in large amounts, any of these drugs has a potential to cause death.

The quantities of these substances prescribed allow for the addict to sell some, offsetting the cost of procurement as well as causing the subject eventual addiction. The time it takes for addiction to take hold is so short that this was one of the main reasons loved ones couldn't believe there was a problem.

The problem is similar for those who use opiates, obtained legally by prescription, to excess in the pre-pill-mill era. Doctors continually wrote prescriptions for pain medications, many unknowingly feeding addictions, not helping pain. For example, people who had had back surgery: as their tolerance for the medication built, they needed larger doses of it to get the same feeling. The classification for these types of pain medication is *narcotic analgesics* (opioids or opiates). People were addicted to these medications but because they obtained them legally, no one realized that there was a problem until it was almost too late. As the quantity and dose rose uncontrollably, the doctor, fearing losing their license, would then discharge the patient. This caused them to seek other treatment or to buy these drugs on the street. You can blame the physician for your loved one's addiction, but the overuse of opiates at that time was *due to ignorance* on the part of the physician. I am not condoning their choice of treatment, but at least their thought process was legitimate. Any doctor prescribing opiates to younger patients today must realize that there is something going on. This is the type of prescriber that the DEA should (and does) go after.

To understand the situation created by the doctor, one must realize that they too are human. We would like to think that to go through the perils and tribulations encountered in becoming a physician the heart and mind must be pure. The fact is, we live in a different world now than when a family practitioner could become wealthy treating their patients. The insurance companies and inflation no longer allow the doctors the profit required to live the lives that they used to. The Physicians Compensation Report in 2015 states that primary care physicians averaged $195,000, and specialists $284,000. In four years, these have increased to $237,000 and $341,000 respectively. While this may seem great, they can no longer afford to live the lifestyle a doctor did back in the 1950s or 60s. This changed once the insurance companies took control of the reimbursements. Doctors once lived a wealthy life. For many it was a way out of poverty and into a high-class way of socialization. Suddenly their world was reduced to that of an average upper-middle to possibly lower-upper income person. This, accompanied by the fact that they had to work much harder to accomplish this, was a source of negativity for many or perhaps some. The doctors had lost control of what to charge their patients.

There was no longer a benefit to being an excellent physician other than the emotional factor that you were a better physician than Dr. Smith, as both were compensated the same for doing the same procedure.

There are those doctors that are happy to help the ill and lead a better-than-average life and then there are those who will do anything to become prosperous. Allow me to say that this is not limited to just the doctor: there are pharmacists that are just as guilty. In fact, in order to survive, most independent pharmacists fill a few of these prescriptions just to pay the rent. It is a sad state of affairs when reimbursement is so limited by the insurance companies that pharmacists must resort to these actions to survive. It is even sadder when your family member becomes the victim of this mess, and ultimately the addict.

We can blame the doctor or pharmacist, but the responsibility rests squarely upon the shoulders of the addict. Nobody forces them to use. Nobody forces someone to walk into a pill mill or seek out a pusher to obtain their drugs. And if your loved one claims it was peer pressure that made them use, then they chose to hang out with the wrong people. So, once again the decision to use rests with your loved one. The important thing for them to keep in mind is that now they must hang with different people. They must look forward, although it is important to keep in mind that, like while driving, you must sometimes look back, too.

I can assure you that most addicts had no intention of ever becoming an addict. It started out with the occasional recreational use of their drug of choice. Those that do not have the potential for the disease of addiction eventually stop using and go on to lead normal lives. Those with the potential for abuse will continue to use and end up deeply embedded in the world of addiction. Continued use for anyone will eventually lead to addiction and once there, you are an addict.

On the upside, as we've discussed, there are those who enter into treatment and eventually remain sober. This time is referred to as "in recovery" and is to be revered. They attend fellowship meetings or any program that they may feel comfortable with and you are there to help your family member. If your addicted family member is serious about recovery, there are people there who will help them along their journey. The first step in the treatment process is to get off the affecting drugs. Next is rehabilitation and this should be followed by either transient living, a halfway house, and/or IOP. They should find, as soon as possible, a meeting place that they like or feel at home in and attend meetings. If they so desire, they may make this meeting their home group. They should find a sponsor as soon as possible as the sponsor is their guide and leader along the path to recovery and through the steps. Most important is that the addict and their family respect this disease. There is a lot of redundancy in this book, but it is there for a reason as the repeated parts are meant to *stress the importance of these sections* in helping you in the support process for your family member and to help guide you through and show you that you are not alone in your experience. You should and must keep in mind that you too, are in need of help as this disease affects the whole family.

Family Interaction

This is a family disease. My personal feeling is that while the addicted family member is in the active phase of addiction, the non-addicted family members are the ones more emotionally affected. Yes, it is true that the addict experiences depression and often despair about their existence as their disease progresses. However, they have the ability to remove themselves emotionally from the situation *by getting high*. The rest of the family is left to face their feelings unprotected and unhelped unless they too choose to self-medicate or perhaps just escape. They must eventually ask themselves how long the act of self-medicating can go on before they are considered addicted. Often they too must seek the help of a mental health professional.

All too often I hear about how a father "must have a drink" of alcohol after work to cope with the tensions of the day (in addition to the fact that they have a loved one suffering from the disease). How would they react if their loved one came home from work stressed, and said, "I have to take an opiate to relax,"? One of the few things about this disease that I still find incongruent is the differing view of drugs and alcohol. Alcohol is a drug that is responsible for one type of addiction. Eyebrows up! This is where I generally get "the looks." What is alcohol? This is a question that raises some controversy. Many alcoholics *do not* consider themselves addicts. They refer to themselves as alcoholics and get resentful if someone refers to them as addicts or especially, drug addicts. But, an addict is someone who cannot exist without using something to prevent entering into a state of withdrawal. If we accept the chemical structure of ethyl alcohol as C_2H_5OH then perhaps this just might begin to appear more drug-like. Once we accept the fact that *alcohol is a drug* then we can accept the fact that an alcoholic is an addict whose drug of choice is alcohol. Why do I refer to the chemical structure of alcohol? Alcohol is a legally obtainable substance. It's socially accepted and abundantly available. You can walk into a grocery store, gas station, or restaurant and obtain alcoholic beverages. Because of this, people tend not to think of it in terms of being an addicting substance.

So, why am I going off on this tangent while discussing family interaction with a loved one's addiction? Because it often occurs in discussions at Family Night; the addict will say that their father can come home from work and gets sloshed "so why can't I?" This brings a response from the using parent that they come home stressed and have a cocktail; this is not addiction. Soon the other parent brings out that this parent stops off on the way home and has a few then comes home and has a few more. So now going back to the parent who comes home from work and has a cocktail to relax, we can see that this is not the doings of an addict unless that drink becomes two and then three drinks and the person must increase their consumption to maintain the feeling that previously, one drink attained. Basically, if you need a substance to assist you to get through your daily functioning then you just might have a problem. Often the parent who chastises the child for using their drug of choice does so while sitting on the couch, sipping their several cocktails, wondering where their child learned to use drugs to ease something that may be causing pain.

One should keep in mind that the addict who is new to the disease is frightened and ashamed and more than likely will not admit to their addiction. They are manipulative and will turn the blame for their addiction on a parent. Perhaps the parent has a drink or two or three in the evening after work, or is a bit aggressive in their parenting. Are they right? Maybe. If the parent's drinking is bothersome (a trigger to the family member who is new or in early recovery) they should keep in mind that they are the one with the disease at this point and they can do something about the situation. An excellent response could be to move into a halfway house. This would allow them to regain their self-esteem by living as an adult on their own. If they choose to remain at home and the action of a parent seems to stimulate the need to get high, the child should speak with another family member or a professional at school and get help. There are resources out there other than self-medicating. I know this sounds like an easy thing but in reality, it is very hard to take that step and could easily result in family problems for the parents. In hindsight, however, these problems are easier to deal with than that of addiction.

Yes, I have heard the bit about "it is the addict's disease and not the family's." This is true, but an addict needs support. This is not the time to stand on principle. So if you happen to enjoy a glass of wine or a beer with dinner *save it for when your loved one is not around* or go out to dinner without them. They are in a very precarious position and just thinking of the house where they used to get high can trigger a relapse. Triggers are a very precarious and often misunderstood part of the disease. My advice to you is instead of trying to figure out why something triggers your loved one, just *accept it as a trigger* and try to avoid doing or saying it. A trigger is something that stimulates a response in the brain of the addict that alters their thinking process (usually negatively).

I attend a family session with a therapist who maintains that not all addicts are affected by the same triggers. She says that you should keep an open line of communication with your loved one so that they feel free to be truthful about what triggers them. They should feel free to address whether or not they feel threatened by the effect of seeing a family member drinking. This may have some merit to it. My feeling is that unless you are going into withdrawal it is the safer path to take by not having a drink at dinner with your loved one even if they say it's okay. Keep in mind that they possibly are still carrying around the shame of their addiction and are not being truthful about their triggers.

When I owned my halfway house, I had a house manager by the name of John. John was an older gentleman in his sixties who had about six years in sobriety. He was what you would call stable. He was very knowledgeable in this field and helped many of the men stay clean who might have otherwise left and relapsed. One day John was scanning the channels on his TV and came upon the show *Drugs, Inc.* He immediately stopped surfing as they were showing a scene in NY where John used to buy and use heroin. This triggered him and thankfully his support group was able to talk him down but for several hours he was ready to walk out and buy some heroin. Why did this happen to someone who was stable and sober for six years and had helped many clients and other people in recovery? It's what those with the disease say is that part of the disease that sits on your shoulder, just patiently waiting for the addict to make the slightest of mental mistakes so that it can pounce down and drag them back into using. A trigger could be absolutely anything. John said when he saw the street on TV, he could *smell the sewer he would sit beside to shoot up*. It could be a song you once heard when high. I know people who fear food shopping because they sell beer and wine in the supermarket. The brain is a marvelous organ composed of long chain amino acids. Sounds simple, but they control every part of the body, producing certain chemicals that can make us feel good or bad. Nobody knows why one thing will act as a trigger for one person and not another.

This disease is both a physical addiction (entailing the detoxification and withdrawal process) and mental addiction (as seen by cravings and triggers). The body produces chemicals known as endorphins. These act on the opiate receptors in the brain to reduce pain and make you feel good. They are involved in our reward circuits and in important activities such as eating, drinking, physical fitness training, and sex. Endorphins may also be involved in boosting self-esteem. When using artificial means—drugs—to produce these euphoric effects, you bring about a cessation of the production of these natural endorphins, so that when you detox, you have to wait for the body to start producing them again. For this reason, very early recovery is an especially risky time for the addict. They may suffer from depression, low self-esteem, and pain. And any of these symptoms could lead to a relapse.

The following is a list of symptoms that occur when one tries to cease using a drug but cannot as they have become physically dependent on it:

- Nausea
- Vomiting
- Diarrhea
- Seizures
- Hallucinations

Symptoms of psychological addiction include:
- Cravings
- Anxiety
- Depression
- Anger
- Fear
- Paranoia

Addictions affect the prefrontal cortex of the brain, the nucleus accumbens, the amygdala, and the hippocampus and involve the neurotransmitters dopamine.

    The brain registers pleasure in the same way no matter what the source of it may be. In the brain, pleasure causes the release of a neurotransmitter, dopamine, that moves the sensation along the nerve receptors. This release occurs in the nucleus accumbens which are located beneath the cerebral cortex. This release is associated with the feeling of pleasure. The nucleus accumbens is referred to as the brain's pleasure center. The hippocampus is responsible for the memories of this pleasure sensation. The amygdala creates a conditioned response to these feelings. The likeliness that addiction occurs is related to the speed at which the dopamine is released, the intensity of that release, and the reliability of that release. Dopamine not only plays a role in in the experience of pleasure but in learning and memory. The current theory of addiction is that dopamine interacts with another neurotransmitter, glutamate, taking over the brain's reward system. This system is linked to our survival system also. Thus we often see our loved one very thin as the need to use has take over their need to eat. Over time, the drug that your loved one uses becomes less pleasurable. This is because the brain responds to the rush of the release of dopamine by producing less or eliminating dopamine receptors.

This accounts for the tolerance as the addict now needs more of the drug to obtain the same effect. The hippocampus and amygdala are responsible for memories of these cues. These memories are what create what the addict refers to as the craving that they experience which may lead, if not properly dealt with, to a relapse.[5]

Supportive siblings can mean a lot to the addict. It is, however, understandable that they might not find them supportive at all. During the active-addiction phase of this disease, the siblings are subjected to many experiences that most people will never know of. Their possessions may be stolen. They may see their family member's name online or in the newspaper in the form of an arrest record. Perhaps they find their sibling passed out on the street. Other friends or family, not realizing that they suffer from this disease, might suddenly become aware of missing possessions. They may overdose at family or friend's houses. After the worry of the possibility of death has passed, the result will be shame. This can result in terminations of relationships as well as humiliation for the sibling. The sibling may be traumatized after seeing their family member overdose.

Past perceptions of this disease have a major role in these feelings of shame. Many still perceive addicts as dirty: an inner-city person who commits crimes to feed their habit and may be violent. Sadly, this may be true, as previously stated, an addict in active addiction does not act rationally. Because of this the disease has an adverse effect upon the family that often causes breakups. This is something that the head of the family should try to avoid by any means. It has happened, to a certain extent, in my family. I have spoken to those siblings that ask for Z to not come to their homes at holiday times. This not only has a negative effect upon the child in addiction but the parent also. The sibling does have the right to not invite their addicted family member to their home. They usually have good reason for this, be it missing items or they want to shield a child from seeing their aunt, high. So what do you as a parent do? You should respect your daughter's request.

---

5   How addiction hijacks the brain. (2011). *Harvard Mental Health Letter*, 1–3. https://doi.org/https://annmacdonalddotnet.files.wordpress.com/2011/07/m0711_final1.pdf

She has a right to invite or not invite who she wants. Z will be hurt but on the other hand, Z can also enter into treatment and decide to stay in recovery. You can have the party in your house; then you can invite who you want.

This is perhaps the reason that, as of recently, many insurance companies have begun to allow extended stays in treatment centers. Previously, the short, twenty-eight-day treatment stays they allowed after the client had completed the detoxification period could be contributable to the large number of relapses that occurred after treatment. Families would, and rightfully so, be apprehensive about this significant failure rate, especially upon the return of their loved ones from one of the many treatment centers. I would often state that twenty-eight days was not actually the correct time allotted to treatment since half of that time was necessary to convince the addict (and perhaps their family members) that the client was actually an addict. This is tedious for the therapist and they are often verbally abused during this time. It also left little time to delve into the reasons they became an addict (and why they would choose to defy the attempts to help them in their recovery).

Perhaps, for some, the so-called addict is correct in their denial of this disease. Could this be a possibility? Yes, most certainly it could be. Let us assume that a parent watches one of the many docudramas that frequent the cable channels. Their loved ones go out on a Saturday night; they have a few drinks, get pulled over by the police and test positive for alcohol or worse. Their car is impounded and they are incarcerated. They are called to the local courthouse, they post bail for them, and are sure that their child or loved one is now one of the many with an addiction problem. The alternative is that the child is an alcoholic or rather an addict and they both, parents and child, think they are just having a wild and good time, kind of a rite of passage.

Scenario two: they go to their court appearance, the judge sits at his desk, the public defender (who has perhaps twenty or more cases to handle that morning) approaches and chats with the judge and the decision reached is that the client should enter into a program that handles addiction problems too and if the client stays clean and attends meetings for six months or one year their record will be expunged. The child and parents or family members gather with the lawyer and are convinced to accept the plea.

The lawyer or a friend or relative knows of this treatment center that did a marvelous job with their child or loved one so you get the phone number and a day later they are in Detox and a week later, in treatment. This is the best scenario. The not-so-best scenario is that now your loved one is going to come in contact with people who really belong in treatment just because he made the bad decision of trying to drive home intoxicated. This decision could possibly be a onetime occurrence if the process of arrest proved to be enough of a lesson to your loved one. Of course, the fact that they have driven under the influence should not ever be taken lightly. If they somehow make it home safely, it is purely a lucky act of fate. Another scenario is an accident involving only damage to the car. More often than not, the accident involves harm to someone or something that could be catastrophic. However stupid this move was on the part of your loved one, it does not necessarily show that they suffer from the disease of addiction.

So now your loved one has made new friends in treatment and is in danger of being tempted to use much more dangerous and deadly drugs, should their new friends suffer a relapse. Having bonded with these new friends over time, they may be less hesitant to experiment with them (assuming that they keep in touch with them) and a relapse occurs. Should they continue along this path the results can be devastating in that addiction could be the resultant end to a possibly innocuous occurrence.

So what does a family member do, should this occur? Approaching a treatment center may sound correct but one must keep in mind that the center is there to keep their census up as this is how their income is generated. I do not say this in a negative manner—many treatment centers are opened by people who have been through hell and back suffering from this disease and because of this have opened a facility to help those who need treatment. They will speak with your loved one upon inception and sincerely try to make a determination as to whether treatment is needed. If, however, your loved one is court appointed, they are going into treatment, end of discussion.

In court, the interview is quick and the person doing the intake depends upon your familiarity with the process. If a treatment center is not the answer, perhaps a therapist is. Again, one must keep in mind that the therapist is dependent upon clients to keep their income on going; therefore a therapist's reviews and track record should be verified and a resonance felt between them and your loved one. This comment is not meant to disparage anyone, especially therapists who initiate many suffering souls on the path of recovery. So, what should one do in a situation such as this? This is a complicated situation and deserves a little time spent trying to think things through clearly. On the one hand the judge doesn't have time to figure out if your child suffers from alcoholism. On the other hand, maybe your loved one doesn't belong in a treatment center with hardcore users where they could possibly be influenced to use.

Treatment facilities, halfway houses, therapists, and doctors that specialize in addiction, like anything else in the real world, consist of those who can help, those who can't, and those who won't. A good place to start is to speak with friends you might know that suffers from the disease of addiction. Look for someone you know that has a decent amount of clean time, someone who has worked a program successfully for a period of time that surpasses a year or so. Call them and explain what has happened and that you would like to get some input. Most important is that you know the person and feel safe both in their clean time and their ability to grasp the situation that you are in. Bring your loved one along with you as it is only they who know what they are experiencing. It is possible that your friend will want to speak with your loved one alone as this is their problem if indeed a problem exists. Please don't get upset when and if you're loved one prefers to speak with this person alone.

Privacy and confidentiality are the basis of this program and what you need at this time is for them to feel at ease, making it easier to be truthful. Remember that guilt and shame are a part of this disease. It is someone who is in a program who can tell when and if your love one is being truthful or manipulating. It is also someone who is in the program who your loved one may feel comfortable enough with to speak the truth to. If it is determined that a problem does exist then your loved one must deal with it either with family input or on their own. Once the person with the problem has reached adulthood, the decisions must be made by them. You as family or friend can only hope to encourage them to do the right thing and should they make the right choice, give your support.

Once again those dirty words surface: denial, guilt, and shame. If you have determined that you want to help your loved one, these three feelings are the toughest barriers to bringing about a positive outcome. You cannot force an adult to do what they refuse to do unless they present as a danger to themselves (suicide) or others (aggressive behavior). You also are not the one who can make the determination of whether your loved one has the disease or just made a bad decision. If you feel that they are indeed in need of help and are on the verge of inflicting harm upon themselves or someone else, you may be able to get them admitted to a program by invoking the Baker Act. This will allow them to be admitted to a facility for a few days during which a psychiatric professional determines their stability. That is the upside. The downside is that often the psychiatric professional is overworked, not well paid for this, and does not have the time or inclination to make a full and accurate determination and at times, your loved one ends up released prematurely. The Marchman Act (in the states of Florida, Washington, California, Alaska, Montana, Colorado, Hawaii, North Dakota, and South Dakota) is another aid for getting your loved one help.

The Marchman Act is a useful tool for someone whose loved one suffers from the disease of addiction. It is used primarily for chemical or substance abuse and allows for involuntary assessment. It permits up to five days for assessment and up to sixty days for successive treatment. Following a petition for involuntary assessment, a hearing is set before a court. Following this hearing, the individual is held for medical stabilization and assessment for up to five days. At this time a second hearing is held for the court to review the assessment. Based on this assessment the judge can then order a sixty day stay in treatment with an extension of up to ninety days. Should the person suffering from this disease leave treatment in violation of the determination of the court they must return to explain why they did not comply. They are then immediately returned to treatment for involuntary care. Should the addict refuse to comply with the order of the court they are then held in civil contempt and ordered to be returned to treatment or to be incarcerated. Yes, the option is theirs. They can choose to turn their life around by entering into treatment and working a proper recovery or be incarcerated. This is a choice that to a person who does not suffer from this disease is a no brainer. To us, this is a simple choice; it is, however, being made by someone who you have no idea of their thought process as they are in active addiction. There is often guilt on the part of the family for the initiation of the Marchman Act. In reality you are initiating a process where an arrest of your loved one takes place so that they may be brought before the court. Your loved one will resent you initially. Most often this is not a pretty scene and your level of guilt is very high. You will ask yourself if you did the right thing. I can only tell you from experience that once your loved one has detoxed and gone through some time in treatment, they are happy that you have acted to save their life. The Marchman Act is not used as a tool for someone who is afraid to confront their out of control loved one. It is used as a last resort when you are sure that if the situation left as is, your loved one will end up dead. At this time, you must and should act and not worry if your loved one will be upset with you.

The Marchman Act: A Step in the Right Direction—Maybe

As discussed, this disease is often harder on the family of the addict than on the addict themself. While in active addiction, they have the ability to soothe their emotions by getting intoxicated. Generally, family members do not have this ability to shelter or deaden their emotions. The government has come out with some legislation to try to assist the family in effort to rein in their loved one should their actions tend toward mental incapacity.

The Florida Marchman Act was passed into law in the year 1993. It is technically known as Florida's Substance Abuse Impairment Act. Although this is a Florida law, most other states have similar law in effect. In Kentucky and in Ohio it is known as Casey's Law. This law gives families the ability to petition the court, asking the judge to commit their family member to treatment. To file, you must complete a form known as The Petition for Involuntary Assessment. This is followed by a hearing that must be set within ten days with a plainclothes sheriff's officer serving the papers to your loved one. The court then hears testimony and will decide if it will enter an order for involuntary assessment. If there is a decision to commit, the judge will decide which treatment center to send your loved one to. Should the patient refuse to go they may be held in contempt and incarcerated.[6]

Let us take a look at how using The Marchman Act can affect the family. With very few exceptions, your loved one is going to become vindictive if they have been involuntarily assessed. They will rant and rave about how they blame you for everything that will or could or has gone wrong in their life. Keep in mind they are now going to have to make a choice between entering into treatment beginning with a period of detoxification, or be incarcerated (thus going through a not-nice detox). Detoxification at best is "not something that someone would enjoy going through." At worst, it can be dangerous and life-threatening, although when properly monitored in a legitimate facility, the resident is usually safe from severe complications.

So now you have entered into the process of invoking The Marchman Act and your loved one has been apprehended by the sheriff's department so things are now in the hands of the addiction professionals. The resentment towards you is proportionate to their fear of withdrawal. What does this mean? Depending upon the feeling that your loved one experiences upon their apprehension they may react differently. One person may be shocked by the arrest while another may become totally irrational and angry, fearing the experience of entering into withdrawal while in lockup. Be prepared for an untoward reaction from your loved one. They may shower you with verbal abuse or sit in stony silence. You have forced the issue probably for the first time since you realized how serious their addiction is and how it has taken control of their life. You have taken this person, who you used to believe to be a free spirit, away from their freedom and are forcing them to make a choice between incarceration or entering into treatment.

You should understand that without the intervention of The Marchman Act, they would choose neither option so now they *must make this choice* with the option of using you as the whipping post. I used the word "freedom" in the previous sentence as

---

6   Wind, Ph.D., B. (2021, June 23). *What is the Marchman Act?* Ask Our Doctors. https://journeypure.com/ask-our-doctors/florida/what-is-the-marchman-act/.

the addict in active addiction would. Is freedom the right term to describe how the person suffering from this disease actually lives while they are in active addiction? Are they ever actually free while they are out there? While I have previously admitted I do not suffer from this disease, does one have to actually experience addiction to realize that living from one fix to the next cannot be considered freedom?

Usually the addict will sullenly or angrily choose treatment over lockup. If you had not initiated The Marchman Act and your loved one used and suffered an overdose and died, you would feel worse then you now do, so try not to feel guilty. It has been my experience that after being in treatment for a short time your loved one will begin to realize that what you did was in their best interest and if this treatment happens to be the successful one, you will be thankful. In fact, even if the treatment ultimately isn't successful, they still most likely will be appreciative of your action. The metamorphosis that your loved one goes through while in treatment is truly something that someone must experience to believe.

They change from a totally irrational person back into the person you once loved. I mention this because not every person suffering from this disease enters a treatment center that is located within traveling distance from where their family lives. If this is the case, you should try to make at least one meeting during their residency so that you may experience your loved one's interaction with the group, the group's interaction with your loved one, feedback toward you and your loved one, and the interaction of the therapist.

The bitterness that you may feel towards your loved one is, for the time being, an understandable emotion. I say this because the things our loved ones have put us through, if we are not educated enough about this disease, are easy to take as a personal attack against us. We spend our life raising our loved one thinking that what we do is loving, and correct. We never think that what we do is interpreted in a totally different way than what we meant. When we go to Family Night meetings we get the chance to express these misconceptions with a therapist and our loved one and hopefully, begin a new perception of how to heal the miscommunication between the family members or loved ones. For example, you may have told your loved one that they are no longer welcome in your house. That could easily be construed by them to mean that you never want to see them again. Yet what you meant was that you can't handle seeing and interacting with them when they are stoned and acting irrational. That statement can bring about a situation where you don't see or hear from your loved one again. Often words are misunderstood, causing pain when you didn't mean to.

A point of interest for the addict to be reminded of is that they weren't really the one to "experience" it. Whoever found them, watched them, heard them, or worried about them (usually a family member), is the one who did. Yes, the client will say that it scared them when they OD'd and perhaps even drove them to enter into treatment, but the fact is they likely collapsed almost immediately, lost consciousness, and truly didn't know what was going on until they regained their awareness. This leaves the family to deal with a comatose (and possibly dead) body to deal with. If you happen to be present when this occurs and have Narcan, you have only a short time to figure out how to use it in order to save a life. You should feel for a pulse and start CPR immediately (if there is none) so that the blood continues to flow to the brain. Administer the Narcan Nasal Spray and get someone to call 911 immediately as paramedics are the most qualified life savers.

Do not worry about your loved one getting arrested as we did. This fear can result in their death. Try to keep a cool head and react in as rational a manner as possible. Easier said than done, I know. You will find that the medics are usually professional, polite, and compassionate, as are the responding police. At this point, they are probably not looking to make an arrest: they are more interested in saving your loved one's life.

You will be surprised by the reaction of your loved one if the Narcan response is rapid as it usually is (if the victim is found in time). It is sort of *Twilight Zone,* revisited. The paramedics will have loaded the patient on a gurney and hooked them up to an IV bag (through which they administer another dose or two of Narcan if necessary). Your loved one will likely sit up like nothing happened, trying to figure out what went down. They may puke once or twice before they smile and wonder when the party started. They are usually taken by ambulance to the hospital where they are observed for a few hours and then released. Upon returning home, their thoughts immediately turn towards leaving and seeking more drugs (opiates) as the Narcan has broken down their body's opiate supply and placed them in a state of withdrawal. But this is just one example of how the overdose can go.

Often the situation is that the addict is with friends who are also high and don't or can't react properly. They may nod out, leaving your loved one there to die, or worse, panic and run. In this case the overdose may result in death, causing despair for the family and for those addicts involved who will have this memory to carry around for the rest of their lives. Hopefully we all only have to deal with the first situation. You now have a loved one (who has just scared you to a point where you no longer suffer from chronic constipation) who is dope sick. They will definitely remember the feeling of dope sickness. Regarding the overdose, they will only remember the stories that they hear from you and a little of what occurred after they regained consciousness. Depending on the thinking process of your loved one, if they have OD'd enough times they might think of entering Rehab but often they feel proud, like they belong to a drug cult. *Don't try to figure out this thinking process as the addict themself can't figure why they think like they do.* Chalk it up to the irrationality of this disease. Quite often you will hear them bragging about how many times they have overdosed when giving input at a meeting or when speaking to friends who also suffer from the disease. Why they would do this is not something they can easily explain, but they do often back down when confronted by the group at a meeting. I blame this on the irrationality of the thinking process of the disease when one is in active addiction.

The upside at this point is that if you move quickly and forcefully enough you can probably get your loved one to enter into treatment more easily than before the overdose. So now your loved one has agreed to enter into treatment. What is going to happen and what can you expect? A lot depends upon your relationship with your loved one prior to their using, the basis for their admission, and how they respond to their treatment. Nothing about this disease is set in stone which is why some people refuse to accept it as a disease. Most diseases present with a certain set of symptoms. The doctor analyzes these, comes to a conclusion, and then begins treatment. Usually there is a positive response, resulting in the person being cured or the disease is put under control.

Initially they enter into Detox. The purpose of Detox is to get the patient off their DOCs in a safe manner so that they can enter into a treatment facility (Rehab) clean and sober. The detoxification process is physically the worst part of treatment. Even when the patient undergoes a "soft landing" detoxification, they still experience cramps, nausea, aches, and perhaps seizures. Fortunately, this is under the watchful eye of a specialized medical professional and you can rest assured that they are safe.

Fortunately, insurance companies have come around to a more practical way of thinking when it comes to this disease. Up until fairly recently, there was a six-or-seven day maximum for Detox. They have finally extended the time allowed for detoxification to allow for the patient to become more stable. The tide is slowly turning towards better treatment for the patient suffering from the disease of addiction.

Yes, this is a deadly disease for which there is no cure but there is treatment. When the addict is in the chronic phase of this disease (acute phase would be in active addiction) it is referred to as being in recovery. Like any other chronic disease, the affected person must work to maintain their recovery. A person suffering from diabetes must take either oral or parenteral medications depending on the type or severity of their disease. Like addiction, diabetes is never cured. Conversely, like a diabetic, an addict is never cured. Initially, certain medications may alleviate their cravings. Over time, the medications are no longer necessary (or their need is reduced), but the addict must maintain their drug free "diet" as they are never more than one use away from a relapse.

Once they have left the treatment facility, the addict needs to maintain their diet by attending meetings, getting a sponsor and a support group, working a program, and ideally continuing treatment with a therapist whose specialty is the field of addiction. Never underestimate the significance of the addiction-knowledgeable therapist. They are a vital part of the recovery process.

The program that the addict chooses is irrelevant so long as they work it passionately. There are many programs that they may find to their liking. The most popular are those that are 12-step based. There are 12-step programs that specialize in male members only or females only. There are groups that specialize in gay membership. Then there are alternatives such as faith-based programs. There are programs such as CoDA that help one work on co-dependency problems. There is also SMART recovery (Self-Management and Recovery Training). This is a mental health and educational program. Life Ring Secular Recovery is for those who don't believe in a higher power. Clearly, there are many post-treatment fellowships available for the addict to choose from. It is up to them to find their place of comfort and then to work that program. I often compare an addict working a program to a student in school: once a student finds their field of choice they begin a journey to learn as much about their future career as possible. The same goes for the addict who begins the journey toward long-term sobriety. Passion is necessary to successfully reach the goal of long-term sobriety. A positive mindset is also key as negative thinking can lead to a relapse. The addict can also move toward a relapse if they have to hear the negative thoughts of family members. Every attempt to enter into sobriety is a unique new trip. Try not to bring up past attempts or incidents that resulted in failure. One never knows which trip to treatment will be the successful one. Your purpose in the recovery process is to remain positive, showing support, while not enabling. A hard concept to grasp for the spouse of someone just out of treatment is that although their thoughts may be about being with you (as they were just away from home for a minimum of thirty days), their thoughts and focus should be centered *on attending meetings and working their program,* as this is what will help them stay in recovery. Your understanding of this is part of the support that they need to succeed.

At this time a hug and "I am so proud that you are working so hard on your recovery. I understand why at this time you are choosing to attend your meeting over spending the evenings with me," will mean more to your loved one than you could believe.

As mentioned, the second phase of treatment is psychological. Your loved one is transferred to Rehab, usually the treatment facility that sent them to Detox (if that was the route that they took to enter into treatment). They must once again go through the admission process, most likely again undergoing drug testing, getting assigned to a room and to, most importantly, their therapist.

Phase two is both hectic and revealing to the addict so you can expect to hear a lot of complaining from your loved one during this phase of treatment. Spa-like with saunas and luxury therapy sessions *this is not*. Usually their day will begin at around 7 am. They shower, get dressed, and tidy their room. The technician in charge then inspects things to make sure that the client has completed their chores.

If you don't hear from your loved one for a while when they first hit Rehab, don't panic. It just means that the facility didn't allow them phone privileges for a certain period of time and then, only if they have been earned. No news at this point is a positive sign as it means that your loved one has done nothing to warrant the facility calling you.

Therapy usually begins at 8 or 9 am and continues until approximately 5 pm. Don't panic, your loved one will not go hungry. In addition to on-site food services, most facilities give them a weekly stipend and take clients to the supermarket where they are allowed to purchase food for the week (under the watchful eye of the technician). As there are four people to a unit, if they use their funds properly, they won't starve.

If, however, they are using the money for inappropriate purposes such as buying soda, cupcakes, chips and salsa, etc., or contraband such as herbals that are forbidden in recovery (or perhaps an illegal substance from the friendly neighborhood pusher who might have figured out that the occupants of the premises are clients of a treatment center), then there will be penalties. If dismissal is necessary, you will usually be contacted but this depends on the age and wishes of your loved one. Remember, your child will always be your baby but the facility is governed by the HIPAA laws and these are strictly enforced. You should have been given a copy of the HIPPA regulations when and if you brought your loved one in to the treatment center. If you call the center they will provide you with this information. As mentioned earlier, they may not have their phone for an indeterminate time. You will feel resentful. They will feel resentful. Almost everyone does. You are feeling a little lost. You are wondering how they are doing or if they are still doing. It is a hard but necessary time. Aside from the previously mentioned reasons for the phone curfew, this is also a time to teach your loved one discipline.

Therapists know how long your loved one has been getting high and living a boundaryless kind of feral lifestyle. Your loved one is now suddenly thrust into a heavily scheduled setting and a totally new living situation. The first few weeks are a kind of hellish situation for them. They are suddenly expected to live drug free, have a routine, a scheduled lifestyle, and to answer to the therapists and technicians who will be controlling their life for the next one-to-three months with days that begin at 7 am and continue until 8 or 9 pm. Until they acclimate to this routine, they probably are better off without your input. If you are able to attend Family Night, that's the best venue for you to discuss your feeling with your loved one as there are therapists, family members, and alumni who can offer their thoughts and experience.

Once phone privileges are restored to the client, you will most likely be high on their list of people to call. Remember that the things you experienced while your loved one was using were the actions and words of the addict, not of your loved one. Try to keep in mind they are two different entities. They probably miss you at this time, especially if it is inconvenient to visit. If you do not live within a reasonable traveling distance to the facility, it is important that you attend a Family Night *at least once*. It is important to let them know that you love them at this time. Another thing to keep in mind is that when your loved one attends a Family Night meeting they can feel alone and ashamed and abandoned for what they have done to you. At this time recovery is still new to them and you should not expect them to act rationally. Although this may be hard for you to do, try not to take their negativity to heart as their actions at this time are something that they will soon regret. As mentioned further back in the book, when they first enter into treatment they are still detoxing and what they say is sometimes not what they mean. The metamorphosis that they go though over time is astonishing. Those who attend the Family Night sessions on a weekly basis will see this.

Your initial impression may be that they enter into treatment, stay for a certain amount of time, and come out cured. But, they attend meetings with a bunch of other addicts who love to use drugs, so how will this help them from going back to using again? You know the old story about birds of a feather so how can hanging out with druggies keep them straight? Low and behold, several weeks or months later your loved one tires of being normal and doing what's right and decides to get high again. Your thoughts concerning your loved one's sobriety can only be corrected by learning more about this insidious disease. It is these addicts who are now in recovery who are one of the keys to your loved one remaining in recovery.

Relapse, Compassion Fatigue, and Putting the Whole Picture Together

Your loved one has been through it all: they got caught, sent to Detox where they withdrew from the drugs, then into Rehab where they hopefully admitted to having a problem. Then ideally they went to a halfway house or sober-living facility and had IOP. Now what? Sometimes it is hard to control your emotions concerning your loved one as now, you see them going back to their old ways and *you cannot do anything to stop their decline.* This is a hard concept to grasp. You are a mother, father, husband, wife, or friend with a significant relationship with an addict. When they were sober they were so easy to talk to. Now they shout and walk out of the room or house instead of having a conversation with you. Sadly, that is how the disease works. Possibly a trained therapist may be able to help if they are sought out early on, but not even they can help in many situations. Those in recovery that are part of your loved one's support group may try to help, but again, *depending on how far the relapse has progressed* they may realize more than anyone that the only solution is to enter into treatment again.

This brings us back to compassion fatigue. Just as the addict suffers from this disease, so do you. I have met addicts who have relapsed more times than you and I have fingers and toes. At that point, you would be so tired of hearing that your loved one is back in treatment or worse, out on the street. Going to treatment could just be their way of getting a clean bed and food for a few months and bingo, they are back on the street. Often this is true. And I can sympathize with you. Let me illustrate what compassion fatigue is. You have put up with the actions of your loved one for a long time. You have tried everything. You have encouraged them to enter into treatment, attended meetings with them, accepted their negative actions (stealing and lying), you put up with the cheating, knowing that it is *not them doing these things. It's the disease.* When they get clean they are so nice and loving. You bought them clothes and nice things, thinking *this time they are gonna stay sober*. Yet, their response has been to relapse time and again and to repeat their cycle of behavior.

You are *done*. No more will you put up with the treatment that you have received from your loved one. *They will never be sober for any period of time*. Let them live with their drugs and whores. You will no longer take their abuse. Yet, if you stop the hysteria, you realize that there is still some love left in you. Often, especially when the addict is your child, what you are feeling is just a temporary emotional process that your brain goes through that allows you to vent—over time it also allows you to cool down and realize that what you are feeling is a natural response to the abuse this disease has put you through.

Once you allow yourself to realize that there is still love for your significant other, your negative thoughts begin to subside. You can once again hug them and offer support. This is usually a time of deep feeling and strong emotional emission. What you have experienced is what a therapist would describe as *emotional fatigue*.

However, it can happen that they (the addicted loved one) are tired of living a life of addiction and are crying out for love and help. If this happens, you should step back and observe how things are progressing. Call the facility and speak with their therapist. Do not offer any financial support at this stage. If they call, speak to them. You might mention that you love them but that you have taken this trip before and you will wait to see what progresses before you accept what they are telling you. Make them earn your trust. If they are doing the right thing, this shouldn't be hard for them.

Remember how I mentioned that the 12-step fellowships have a reward system (as do most other programs)? It may be a token, chip, or keychain: ask your addict what color token they have. Do not be surprised if they get resentful about you asking questions concerning their sobriety. They have been through a lot and can't quite understand why you won't trust them at this stage of sobriety. Do not feel guilty. As previously stated, trust is something that must be earned. It comes with time but may never be completely obtainable. Remember this is an incurable disease. There is always that chance of relapse, although as time progresses and your loved one continues to work a proper program, that chance decreases. Trust can be rebuilt slowly over time.

You have a right to experience compassion fatigue. You have been through as much as your loved one, only you had to do it without the ability to numb your thoughts and emotions by using intoxicants. However, as Malachy McCourt once said, "Resentment is like taking poison and waiting for the other person to die." Remember that when it comes to your loved one, life should be treated in the same way as you would drive your car: you must at times look into your rearview mirror to see what's behind you. However, if you're constantly looking back there, you will surely end up in an accident. What your loved one has done *is now in the past* when they are in recovery, and they usually carry the shame for it. I often tell addicts (at meetings) that what they have done is in the past, it cannot be changed, and they must look to the future. Understanding this concept is where having an addiction therapist and a good support program can do so much to aid your loved one's journey.

The addict's first major success in the reward system is the one-year-clean medallion. There are minor goals long the path (30-, 60-, and 90-days-clean medallions), that are stepping stones to give the person in recovery encouragement along their first-year-clean journey. Let your loved one know that you are proud of their accomplishment—buy them a cake and celebrate.

Though the 12-step programs seem to be the most effective of the programs, perhaps it is *because* they are the most prevalent they are the most effective. But there are many other programs out there that work just as well. Regardless of the program they choose, the most important thing is for your loved one is to *work a program with passion*. They must find the program that they feel the most comfortable with. Your encouragement is helpful but this is a strange time in the life of the recovering addict.

Yes, they want and need your support, but at the same time they may be resentful if you enter into their space. This is a time where confusion is common. Do not take what the addict says personally. So many times I have seen big tough clients crying for what they have done to their loved ones. Some of these clients will make it and some will relapse. A lot depends on how the addict feels and if they work their program. There are those who have convinced themselves that they can only stay sober for a certain amount of months and then they always relapse. This is what the therapist has to deal with. Sometimes good input may help, but usually these feelings are deeply rooted and that may be considered part of the disease and why treatment centers are such a necessary part of recovery. I can often be heard pointing out that their insistence of "only being capable of staying sober for a few months," is bogus. It is simply their way of rationalizing their relapse. I compare it to someone taking algebra but not doing the necessary work to pass the course. When they flunk, they say, "I am a terrible math student and can never pass, no matter how many times I take it." Hmmm…perhaps working at it might have helped?

The third phase of treatment, for those who choose it, involves living in a recovery residence or halfway house. They have been through the detoxification process and completed Rehab, which included therapy, and helped them learn how to take care of themselves. The assigned therapist would have helped them find out why they did what they did: what led them into a world that could only destroy them and their loved ones? Hopefully this has been revealed and addressed, as this is when your loved one moves into a residence run by someone who should have had a protracted length of time in recovery. Clients are required to sign a lease and agree to follow rules and regulations of the house. They are required to maintain a clean residence and do their own laundry. They must shop, cook, and clean up after themselves. They are encouraged to attend meetings, get a sponsor, attend house meetings and be in by a certain time (a curfew). They have completed the technical part of treatment and this third aspect is strictly voluntary (but a significant part of treatment).

They have likely lived for too long without having to answer to or respect anyone, pay bills, or be responsible for anything. Thus, the purpose is to reacquaint the addict with how to function as a person in the real world in everyday life as they are no longer under the strict supervision of either their therapist or technician. Although life in treatment is not always fun, it is a protected environment where they can seek help when certain feelings (especially the urge to use) become overbearing. Though structured, halfway homes leave the addict more freedom, so hopefully they are well enough not to abuse it.

Pressure to do the right thing can be applied by members of their fellowship in ways that your loved one does not resent. "Don't keep checking up on me!" might be the response you get when asking how their meetings are going, whereas the halfway house roommate might get a positive response such as, "Hey I found a great sponsor! They've been sober a long time, seem assertive yet companionate, and it's very easy to speak to them." This does not mean that you have no place in your loved one's recovery, nor that you shouldn't ask questions. Just be aware that there may be better, more trusted people out there for your loved one to confide in at that time than you.

Am I Helping or Enabling?

So what role *do* you play in their recovery? This question stumps many a loved one and is especially hard for the parents of an addict to answer. For years they have been helping their loved one to survive by supporting them financially, giving them a place to live, perhaps making car payments—surely they must have a car to get to work, when and if they find a job! There are so many things that you have done to help your loved one get back on their feet that the idea that this "help" could be *the reason that they haven't gotten back on their feet* never occurred to you. This is the time to tell you: your addicted loved one does truly love you. This is an irreversible truth that many a family member may not believe. Just as you know your love for them is unconditional, so too is their love for you. The major difference is that you do not suffer from a disease that distorts your thinking to the point that all you can think about is where you can get your next fix. It's not a choice they have at this point.

Yes, this is a disease that is sometimes referred to as "a disease of choice" and there was a time they could choose, but at this point in active addiction, being able to choose is in the rearview. Us Normies have no idea how the mind of a dope sick addict thinks or works. So when you give your loved one $10 for a pack of cigarettes, just maybe that money is going for a bag of heroin. That car payment you made for them just might be freeing up some cash to buy drugs to use or sell or both. The fact that you give them a place to sleep just might be helping them to avoid hitting their rock bottom. Are these written in stone under the enabling heading? Absolutely not! One major reason to help the addict move to a halfway house after they complete treatment is to avoid being the enabler. Instead, you are encouraging them to mature and make decisions for themselves.

Very seldom does your loved one appreciate *your* anxiety concerning their recovery. You have earned the right to be concerned. Often anxiety can be alleviated by a simple phone call if they have been "off the radar" for awhile and you are worried. This not only helps you, but also helps them. An amazing part of the addict's life is that they always seem to be able to obtain a cell phone. They may end up sleeping on a bench, searching through garbage cans or dumpsters for food, but they always have a cell phone—and oh yes, tattoos. Unless you are asked to pay for these, you should not ask questions about them. It has something to do with their concept of self-esteem while they are in active addiction. This often carries over to their sobriety.

Back to that helpful phone call to check in on them: they may initially resent your questions. "I love you," is a good way to start the conversation. To backtrack for a moment, why all this discussion of anxiety and a phone call being helpful? To give a concrete example, imagine your loved one goes to meetings every evening from 8 until 9 pm, and are usually home by 9:30. This has been their routine for the past few weeks, but now it's 10:30 pm, you haven't heard from them, and panic has set in.

You are pacing and peeking out the window every five minutes. Finally, you hear the car pull into the driveway! You head to the door to greet them and—sure that they have relapsed—ask where they have been. In return, you get a look of disdain. They storm away to their room, slam the door, and leave you standing there alone, upset, and ready to throw them out of the house. Were you wrong to act like this? Were you being unreasonable? Were your actions irrational? Your loved one may think so, but were they?

Depending on what you have previously been through or what you might have agreed upon when they moved back into your residence, the answer to those questions is most likely no. In this situation, even if you had been calm, you would have received a similar response. The response of frustration or disdain is common: they entered treatment and completed the program. They are going to meetings and are working a program. They feel that a certain amount of trust should be there. Are they right? To a point, they are. However, a simple phone call explaining that they were going to be late would have gone a long way. You would have been overjoyed to hear that after the meeting they had spoken with some of the members of the fellowship who noticed that your loved one seemed to be serious about their recovery so they asked them to go for coffee to discuss their program. This is referred to as "fellowshipping" *and is a big step toward long-term recovery*. Your loved one was doing the right thing but forgot that there was someone at home living in constant fear of them relapsing. A phone call would have taken a few seconds of their time and whoever they were fellowshipping with surely would have understood.

Communication is an important part of recovery. Your loved one was excited about being accepted by the group and didn't think about the effect it would have on you (or was living in the moment!). They possibly expected to return home to tell you how proud and excited they were that some people from the meeting had invited them to fellowship and were heartbroken to receive your anger and fear. Your conclusion that your loved one had relapsed would be upsetting to them.

You might wonder what would have occurred had this happened if they were living in a halfway house. Believe it or not, the situation would not have been handled that differently. The house manager of a halfway house usually resides at the residence. Remember those papers they had to sign along with their lease? They state that there are curfews set for the residents, and the house manager speaks with each incoming resident and explains that, should a situation arise where they will be late *they must call to inform* him (boundary). The house manager will usually request that the resident stop at his room to do a drug test to make sure that they are still clean. There are certain exceptions to this rule and a good house manager should be able to recognize when a relapse is looming vs legitimate tardiness. They will act upon this knowledge in an attempt to prevent the relapse. A definite advantage to your loved one being in a halfway house is that an experienced house manager has a much better chance of picking up on the signs of relapse (and possibly preventing it) than you would.

After a period of time, depending on the behavior of your loved one, you will be allowed to visit them and discuss any apprehensions that you may have with the house manager. As long as your loved one has given their permission, the manager should be more than willing to discuss your loved one's progress with you. But, don't take it personally if they have not granted you access: it is common for addicts to want privacy. Over time, this need to be private will diminish and you will eventually regain the intimacy you once had.

The Journey Toward Long-Term Sobriety

Since I have shared our experience with our daughter, I will update you as to where she is emotionally and how she currently affects the family at the time of this writing. I do this with her consent—assuming that she still remembers that she has given me this permission. As I have previously stated, my daughter is beautiful with above-average intelligence. To say that our family is proud of her achievements would be an understatement. She has many qualities that should have led her to a successful life and career.

From what she has admitted to, she started using drugs around the age of twelve. She began smoking pot and popping an occasional Xanax, an anti-anxiety agent in the drug classification known as benzodiazepines. Gradually, the pot smoking progressed to a point that she was became emotionally addicted to it. The use of the Xanax (alprazolam) progressed and she became physically and emotionally addicted to it. This type of drug, unlike heroin, gradually sneaks up on the user who usually has no concept that they are becoming addicted until they try to stop using.

At that time, I had no idea at all that this problem existed. Although, as a licensed pharmacist I should have had some knowledge of what was evolving; as a parent, I suffered from the disease known as denial She was young and I was naïve as to what addiction was about. Later on, as her marijuana use became more obvious, I confused what she was doing with the sixties era I grew up in. It was a period of protest, intellectualism, and getting high to celebrate.

I must put most of the blame on the fact that I would not allow myself to understand the extent to which the use of drugs had progressed from the smoking of a simple joint at a party to the use of life-destroying opiates and benzodiazepines. I am not really sure what drug was her initiator: if she started with the pot or the Xanax. At this point for her, it really doesn't matter. What does matter is that at a very young age, my daughter could not live without pills. You should be aware that for a young child there is a significant difference between smoking pot and taking benzos. So try to keep track of what you are seeing. Neither is a good choice but there is a difference.

I was running a somewhat difficult business and didn't see the signs of her problem. I did notice that her grades were declining but was too busy to take the time to fully figure out what was going on. Truthfully, and this is one of the hardest things for a parent to admit, I probably took the easy way out and chose not to see the signs of her progression toward addiction. It is so much easier to bury your head in the sand and figure, "this phase will pass as it does for so many others." It is also true that it is not always easy to pick up on the signs of drug use. This is especially true with the new affluence—often our children have a television in their room and a $1000 phone in their hand so now our contact with them is at best, minimal.

When she was about to enter into her senior year of middle school, we moved into a new house in an affluent city in South Florida. I believe it was at this time that she began her downward spiral. She was sneaking out of the house at night and getting high at a neighbor's house. There was little that my wife or I could do to control her. She would open the window, remove the screen and go down the block to her friend's house to indulge in a few hours of getting high. She somehow got through high school, which was a relief, and started attending a local college. She then transferred to the Art Institute where she seemed to not only do better academically, but was a happier person. All the while, unknown to her mother and me, her addiction was steadily progressing. This I can only guess was masked by her happy external appearance and her good grades. I am guessing that it was around this time that she became hooked on the opiates. I am sure that there were signs but as the addict is a master at covering up their addiction, so too are parents masters at not seeing what is right in front of them when it comes to their loved one. The truth is that the addict could not tell you exactly when they become addicted as this could have been something that had been going on for a while—until they develop their first case of dope sickness, they don't know that they are addicted.

She graduated with honors, which further hid her addiction. Her decline was a steady one, however, and it was only a matter of time before something happened that brought the whole mess out into the open. It was soon after graduation. She had broken up with her boyfriend who had returned home (and eventually ended up marrying a local girl).

Anyway, it was only a short time that she was shooting the Blues (slang for oxycodone). She went through treatment and seemed to be one of the winners. She seemed to be doing well for a few months. But it was not to last. The fact that it didn't last is not all that unusual as we now well know that there is an extremely high rate of relapse with this disease. The high rate of relapse is in no way a comfort to the family member should this occur. It is normal at this time to feel confused, depressed, and any other emotional feelings that may arise. This is especially true for the loved ones of the first-timer (that was us that day) who, despite what they are told, deep down feel that relapse is something that "only happens to the other families."

There, in treatment, she met and made friends with clients that used heroin. Yes, this is always a possibility when your loved one enters into treatment. You will initially want to put the blame on someone, so you'll blame the facility for this. Remember again that *no one is responsible for your loved one's addiction other than your loved one*. You should neither accept the responsibility for an addict's use nor the credit for their successes. This is something that only an addict can do for themselves. Treatment can help them to figure out why they feel as they do or why they use and the programs can help them to reach the decision to stay clean and sober. But ultimately, it is only the addict that should be credited with being willing to do what is necessary to maintain their sobriety.

My daughter has been through three treatments so far and none were successful for her. The fault rests with her and not the treatment centers, although she would like to divert the blame toward someone or something else. The fact is, she went to a wonderful facility that can boast of many successes. A treatment center can only contribute to the sobriety of a patient if the patient is willing to work with the facility. I compare it to a person who develops pneumonia and goes to see their physician. The physician does a work-up, concludes that the patient is ill with bacterial pneumonia, and hands the patient a prescription for an antibiotic, a cough suppressant, and a bronchodilator. The patient leaves the office, throws the prescriptions in the garbage, and two weeks later dies from the disease. The family berates the doctor for the loss. Clearly, the reality is that the patient was at fault for not taking their medication. When dealing with the disease of addiction, the therapist, their program, and support system are their antibiotics, cough suppressant, and bronchodilator. It is the patient, the addict, that must choose to take their medication.

However, the journey toward long-term sobriety is a lot more intricate than just having to remember to take medication to recover. It is an emotional disease with many aspects to the recovery process. Even the addict who is serious and passionate about their recovery will have a long and arduous journey ahead of them. This journey is obviously more than my daughter was/is willing to commit to at this time. We can never tell when the time will be right for her.

You may develop compassion fatigue and wish that your loved one would move to another planet and lose your phone number. I receive mail addressed to Z from collection agencies, the police, and the court system on a weekly basis. My wife often throws it away and we constantly have to tell callers that she does not reside with us any longer. We never know when or if she is going to call or show up at our doorstep. When she does, we enjoy the visit or conversation, knowing perhaps that what she tells us is often not truthful. We do know that she is our daughter and that our love for her is unconditional.

When she is sober we enjoy her visit more. When she is totally stoned and acting incoherent, we try to shorten her visit. When and if the times comes that she is ready to get sober for real, and we are still around to give her support, we will be there for her. I do know that if she doesn't overdose or succumb to this insidious disease in another way, she will someday get tired of living as she does and enter into treatment and recovery for good. I know that when she does there will be people in the fellowship she chooses who will be there for her, wonderful people who know and understand exactly what she has been through. When my daughter and your loved ones are ready to begin their journey, people will be there to offer support and aid in their recovery.

Be forewarned: those in already in recovery will initially show some skepticism/hesitation to interact with a new person who is suffering from this disease and trying to get clean. This is because sobriety is a precious and often fragile state for those in recovery and someone who constantly relapses can be a trigger to others. Therefore, there may be hesitation to accept your loved one initially, until the others see that he/she is serious about their recovery (trust is built). Then they will be there as a support network for them. This is not to say that they will not be there for you. As they say at their meetings "the newcomer is the most important part of their fellowship." They would like to see your loved one show up at a meeting more than once though.

If your loved one Googles NA they will see that they are there to help the newcomer so perhaps I have given you the wrong impression when I say they would first like to see if the newcomer is serious about their recovery. Both happen to be true. Yes, they say come to a meeting even if you are not clean. They will give support. They follow this up by saying that your loved one should keep coming back but should come back clean. They continue to say that your loved one does not have to wait for an overdose or jail to come to a meeting, their doors are open. When I say they "wait to see if you are serious about your recovery" what I mean is there are those that come for the coffee and to socialize. These meeting are serious and if your loved one keeps showing up stoned, drinks coffee, and leaves, showing no sign of wanting to enter into sobriety, they will notice this and stand back. The fact that they keep coming back could indicate more than just wanting a cup of coffee or to socialize. So they will continue to give him or her a chance to get clean. They will talk to them. Their attention will be directed toward those that are serious about sobriety.

I still attend two Family Night meetings per week. I do this for a few reasons. First, so that I can continue to gain knowledge of this disease and give intelligent support and input to the clients of the two treatment centers where I attend meetings. Second, to help support the many clients who enter into treatment from out of town and have left home feeling as though their families no longer want any kind of interaction with them. They have hurt their loved ones, stolen from them, lied to them and brought shame upon their families. I try to build up to an interaction with these clients, explaining that yes, it may take a while to mend those feelings brought on by their past behaviors but for the most part they have to look forward as their recovery can be the great mender of those broken fences. For the most part, these anxieties or apprehensions are one-sided on the part of the addict. It has been my experience that most often, working passionately on long-term recovery is a great healer (along with working a program). There is a time and a place for your loved one to try to make amends should those fences be high enough to have shut the addict out. The 12-step programs cover this. Steps eight and nine are about making amends and repairing relationships damaged by the actions of one while in active addiction. The third reason I go to these meetings is to show my constant support for Z.

Z often disappears for long periods of time. Sometimes months pass before we hear from her. Emotionally, this affects us in a negative way, but as time passes we have grown somewhat accustomed to these voids. Yes, we always wonder if she is well; these feelings are only natural, but over time I have gained the knowledge that allows me to survive and I use this to help my wife deal with her emotions. We both know that should something happen, we will be contacted by the authorities. This knowledge comes from the fact that when she gets into trouble they do contact us. We know not to take this void time personally as she is out on a run and when she comes back in, she contacts us and is warm and loving once again. This isn't something that you learn on your own. This is knowledge I have acquired over time through my friends in recovery, from the clients in the treatment centers, and from experience with Z's addiction. Over time, you can learn to deal with a Z in your life, but after thirteen years of dealing with my situation, when the phone rings late at night, I still fear someone is calling to tell us that Z is in hospital or jail.

Initially, our big fear was always that she had overdosed and died, which was why we hadn't heard from her. We have had various visits and calls from the police (both the local and non-local precincts), so should something bad occur, they know how to reach us. We do know that right now, she is somewhere in Miami and is well known in the system. I can tell this by the court correspondence that we often receive. To a family new to this disease, I am sure this sounds a little crazy and cold, but it is our only way of knowing that she is still okay. In this case, bad news is good news. We do worry as we open the envelopes, fearing that there might be the ultimate in bad news, but this too becomes a way of life. It by no means affects our love for her.

The good news, and this too may sound a little insane to the family members who are new to this, is that with the spread of the epidemic and its negative affect on the more affluent communities, treatment of the sufferers will and is becoming better. More money will be allotted for research; there will be more scrutiny of the facilities, thus filtering out those in it for the money and not the success of their clients, and there will be a better focus on prevention rather than mainly recovery.

For now, the government and insurance companies, having little knowledge of the disease of addiction, treat it as a disease of choice and habit. We know that it can start out as one of choice but quickly becomes a psychological and emotional disease. For this reason it is not one that can be cured in a specific amount of time or for that matter, ever. It can be controlled and this is one of the hardest factors for a loved one or even an addict to comprehend.

This may sound depressing to family members initially. This is why I strongly recommend that the family attend meetings too. As I have previously mentioned: this is a family disease. It affects the family as badly, if not worse, than it affects the addict when they are in the active phase of addiction. We too need help and should never be ashamed to seek that help. There are free meetings out there. They are there to help you. The people who attend these meetings have gone through or are going through the same thing that you are and are at these meetings because they too need help. If you allow yourself to accept the help and education that is attainable at these meetings, you will greatly benefit from them. Take advantage of the opportunity that these meetings present. I have often heard people complain that they found them objectionable. You should, however, try to attend *at least six meetings before you make your decision.* You should also try different meetings as you might find one objectionable and another more to your liking. I personally found that the Family Night meeting was more to my liking and as I became more active with learning how to deal with the disease, I also attended open NA meetings.

Your loved one does not intentionally try to be your source of pain. These actions are brought on by the disease. I have seen, many times, the client try to place the blame for their addiction on their loved ones. Don't take this personally. We are usually victims of our upbringing and we allow this to influence how we react to different circumstances. This affects how we raise our children and react to certain stimuli. It is quite often the cause of conflict between our addicted love one and us. For example, my parents brought my sister and I up in a strict manner. We had to be in bed at a certain time. Education was pushed upon us as the way to achieve success and gain respect. I think I was in my late thirties before I admitted to my parents that I smoked pot back in the sixties. At the time, I resented them for this. I now see that I have retained many of their values as I too pushed my children (but not my grandchildren) to get a better education. The job of raising my grandchildren is deferred to their parents; I may make suggestions should the opportunity present itself.

Treatment will help your loved one find their own way as well the key as to what stirred up these feelings. Remember, the drug is *just the symptom* of the disease; the disease is more about why your loved one has to use drugs to get through the day. When you feel that you can't deal with things, step back. If you do attend meetings, call someone in your support group or your sponsor if you are in a fellowship designed for family members.

I often tell the clients that the sayings that are familiar to us all did not come about by chance. They usually came into being over time through life experiences. Sayings such as "Hindsight is 20/20," sounds so simple but you can see the brilliance of those few words. Bill didn't sit down in front of his typewriter and write the Big Book. Rather, he and others got together and *through their combined experiences* wrote this now world-renowned guide to help people maintain their sobriety. So the saying that "Hindsight is 20/20" came into being due to someone's life experiences.

Meetings are often closed with the recitation of the Serenity Prayer. It is said so frequently that one can tend to take it for granted. Think of the wisdom of this prayer:

> *God, grant me*
> *The Serenity*
> *to accept the things I cannot change,*
> *The Courage*
> *to change the things I can, and*
> *The Wisdom*
> *to know the Difference.*

I cannot promise you that you will ever live a perfectly normal existence if you have someone who suffers from the disease of addiction in the family. But, there is help available for you. The help does not just happen for you just as recovery does not just happen for your loved one. Like any new skill, you have to put in a certain amount of effort to succeed at it and this will come with time. It won't likely take as long if your loved one is in recovery.

But, even if your loved one isn't in recovery yet, with the help of your fellowship or a therapist, and your willingness to learn about the disease, you should be able to achieve a certain level of peace.

Your loved one loves you and the shame and guilt that they feel for the pain that they have caused you is difficult for them to overcome. As I have previously mentioned, it is helpful for you to look forward and support their recovery from this point on. Yes, you sometimes must look back, but it serves no purpose to bring up the past if it brings negative results into your loved one's recovery. You are entitled to remember what you went through while your loved one was in active addiction, but to bring it up to them could be harmful. They know what they have lived through and put their family through.

Google is a valuable tool that may allow you to find help. Simply type "addiction help for the family" and a world of information should pop up on the screen. The same goes for NA and AA meetings. Look for a listing of an open meeting in your area and try to attend. You will see that there is world of people out there who are going through the same emotional ups and downs that you are. They are willing to assist you along your journey.

I wish you the best. Never give up! The success rate is improving as the treatment centers are becoming more knowledgeable in their treatment of this disease.

Is the Epidemic Really New?

We speak of this "sudden explosion of heroin addiction" as a new epidemic. In 2013, the U.S. Attorney's Office identified and responded to a major increase in health care crisis in northern Ohio. Cuyahoga County, Ohio saw a 1000 % increase in opioid deaths between 2007 and 2016. According to Health and Human Services, 760,000 people have died since 1999 from a drug overdose. Those of us who raised our children in good homes and good neighborhoods are finding the epidemic shocking—it *is* hitting our neighborhoods.

We knew that there was such a thing as heroin addiction, but it was something that was far away from our reality. Perhaps a neighbor or two sometimes spoke about their child in college, saying, "All she/he does is get high," or, "This is just a college thing and I'm sure that once they graduate, they'll get a job, meet someone, and start a family." Or even, "You know, it's just a 'rite of passage' type thing." Yes, there were those in the burbs who did became addicted to drugs other than alcohol. They were in the minority and it was kept secret so unless it was a close friend of the family or a family member, no one knew of the situation.

Drug use was, for the most part, limited to the beat generation of the forties and fifties, and started to become popular in the sixties. According to the Recovery Research Institute, it was the in the sixties when heroin use began to become more commonplace in the middle and upper-middle class population in the US. After the tumultuous times of the sixties and seventies, most people reverted to a somewhat normal, functional family style of living, although they often continued to smoke marijuana. As they grew older they would sit and talk about when, away at college, "Yeah, ya hadda study but the parties were so much fun," or perhaps for those that didn't attend college it was just "the good old days." For some, however, the result was different. They didn't slow their drug use and thus we saw the emergence of a slowly progressive epidemic.

When was the beginning of the opiate explosion though? We have to go back to the sixties or probably before then to see when this epidemic actually began. The Vietnam War was not just fought in the jungles. It seems that heroin was readily available for our soldiers in the back streets of the cities where our bases were located, should they have chosen to deal with the stress that they faced on a daily basis by self-medicating. Many of our soldiers first came in contact with heroin in the back streets of Saigon and returned home fully addicted to this drug. The government's response was to discharge those soldiers. The Veteran Administration hospitals were understaffed and not trained to deal with this problem.[7]

Where I live in Broward County, Florida, there is only one government treatment center for the whole county. The Broward Addiction Recovery Center (BARC) handles the second most populous county in the state of Florida with a population of 1.953 million people. The amount of drug-related deaths in the state of Florida had increased from 2,175 in 2014 to 4,672 in 2016.[8] One can only try to guess how many drug-related death went unreported. I can attest to the fact that if the death was drug related, it is often covered up. With most addicts in active addiction not

---

[7] On a related note of interest: In 1971, Veterans Affairs Hospitals only handled three referrals out of 12,000 heroin-using servicemen. For this reason, we saw a sudden influx of veterans returning home and living on the street. Many still tend to look at the homeless sleeping on the street with disgust instead of fighting for more government treatment centers. With the current epidemic there is more help now available for these veterans.

[8] FL-DOSE Program (Dr. Karen Card, Principal Investigator): http://www.floridahealth.gov/statistics-and-data/fl-dose/program-components.html

having insurance, one can see how the need for more facilities is necessary when you consider the fact that BARC has a fifty-bed capacity under normal circumstances, that was reduced to twenty-eight when the Covid-19 pandemic hit. The center happens to be, as far as government-owned facilities are concerned, one of the finest in the state. They are truly state of the art. They have a fifty-bed Detox center and a ninety-plus-bed treatment center. There is, however always a wait list to get into the facility, which is hazardous as an addict seeking treatment can change their mind at any time. The drug problem in Broward, as in most major counties, is the drug problem at large. Although there are other facilities, they are privately owned and without insurance, hard to gain admission to.

The decision to enter treatment can change at the drop of a hat. There is often a wait of several days to several months at the county facility, or at best, definitely hours (prior to the pandemic). Now during the pandemic, many people who wish to enter into treatment have to wait up to a month or two to get into the county facility, as I hear from the people I know when I attended NA meetings. As previously mentioned, it can take less than a second for an addict to change their mind about getting help. People I know tell me you now put your name on a list and they call you when a bed becomes available. This sadly gives the patient able time to change their mind as this can take weeks or months, depending on how long the list is, and if those on the list are still interested in entering into the facility.

A major cause of the spread of this disease was the lack of concern as most people felt this epidemic was confined to the inner city. I am using the term "inner city" as a euphemism for the Black and Hispanic communities in the lower socio-economic neighborhoods of our cities. We never considered that many diseases spread and that we and our loved ones would someday become infected by what we considered a choice not a disease, made by those with little education, living in poverty—those we would never come into contact with. Well, as diseases tend to spread when people and the government don't care, it did, and now it is considered an epidemic. In the midst of the Covid-19 pandemic and we can see the reaction the populace has had. Perhaps if the reaction to the heroin problem back in the 1940s, 50s, and 60s had been similar, we could have avoided this current epidemic. Even now that the heroin epidemic has infiltrated the burbs, there are still those that don't believe that it is part of the disease of addiction.

People have a funny outlook about this disease. Some drink nightly to excess but because alcohol is available legally almost anywhere, they feel comfortable in their alcoholic situation. They most likely do not consider themselves a substance abuser even though they may have several drinks on the way home from work and several more after dinner, each and every night. I have often seen them at Family Night meetings, wondering how their child could have entered into the world of addiction, coming from such a wonderful background.

Should they continue to go to meetings at the treatment center, I can see how they, if willing to open their eyes, could slowly become aware of the fact that maybe they too have a problem and—just maybe—genetics may play a part in this disease. After all, an alcoholic is an addict whose drug of choice happens to be alcohol. Maybe this disease has been around longer than we think, but maybe we have just managed to avoid driving past the areas equivalent to the Bowery—a section of Manhattan that had many hotels considered flop houses and attracted those suffering from addiction who often slept in the doorways of the stores.

The other night I was in a semi-shocked state after a client asked the therapist if during their church service the sipping of the wine would be considered a relapse. She hesitated with her answer but eventually gave the correct one. Those that suffer from this disease may never again partake in the consumption of any substance that has the ability to trigger them or induce a euphoric effect. In this case, the reason for the consumption may appear innocent enough. However, there is a better chance than not that the person suffering from this disease will eventually find themselves attending services more and more frequently until they realize that their presence in church has become more than for the purpose of religious enlightenment.

We would replace the bottle of kosher wine with grape juice to try to prevent a trigger for those in the family that suffer from this disease. It was appreciated, but now as I think about the situation, did this really not present as a trigger? Often, it is not only the ingesting or using of the substance but also the act of the consumption or the mimicking of the previous stimulus that also is the trigger. We must do what we think is right, but it is important to consult with those that suffer from the disease and at least let them know what is going to be at a function rather than to let them face it at the function with no warning.

Getting back to the topic of when this epidemic may have started, I believe that one of the reasons is that there are those that who stubbornly refuse to accept it as one. If all had accepted it as a disease, perhaps we could have limited the amount of those who became addicted initially. The addict initially made the choice to use and it was that choice that led to their becoming addicted. Sadly, it is no longer a choice on the part of the addict to use once they have crossed the line and entered into the world of addiction. So, yes at one time it may have been a choice.

Some people ask, once the client leaves the Detox facility isn't it once again a choice? To a certain extent this is true but we should keep in mind that the brain is both an illogical and a very logical organ. The cerebral cortex, the nucleus accumbens, the hippocampis and the amygdala are all involved. The brain recognizes pleasure in the same way, regardless of the stimulus. A pleasurable stimulus causes the release of a neurotransmitter known as dopamine in the nucleus accumbens which is located just beneath the cerebral cortex. This release of dopamine is so connected with the pleasure sensation that neuroscientists refer to this area as the brain's pleasure center. Addictive drugs have a shortcut to the brain's reward system by flooding the nucleus accumbens with dopamine. This creates an overreaction in the pleasure center. The hippocampus creates the memories of this rush of pleasure while the amygdala creates a conditioned response to certain stimuli: the pleasure created by the addictive drugs being of high priority. The likelihood that a drug will be addicting is related to the speed of the release of dopamine, the intensity of the release, and how reliable that that release is.

New research has shown that the dopamine does not act alone. It interacts with glutamate, taking over the brain's system of reward-related learning. This system is life affecting as it rivals the normal survival system. This makes us go after the stimulus. Over time, the brain adapts to the pleasure feeling, causing the addict to need more to achieve the same feeling. As defined in the July 2011 *Harvard Mental Health Letter*, this is known as *tolerance*.

But often there is a familial factor, too. If the family comes to meetings when the addict enters into treatment, we often find that there is a history of addiction in the family. Perhaps they don't share the same addiction. Perhaps the client has an addiction to drugs and has a parent who is a compulsive gambler or eater. We may find that a parent had a parent who also suffered from a compulsive disorder. In that case it is possible that the client would have ended up suffering from an addiction, regardless of whether it was to drugs.

Drug addiction is unique in that it is not just caused by a compulsive disorder. It is much harder to enter into remission should one suffer from this as well as an addiction. As further explained in the *Harvard Mental Health Letter*, in the case of a drug having the potential for addiction, biochemical reactions produced in various portions of the brain as previously discussed have the effect of permanently altering the structure of the brain, thus causing the abuser of these substances to enter into a state of addiction forever. And, as explained in "Drugs Shatter the Myth" published by the National Institutes of Health, the neurotransmitter dopamine is released in response to pleasure—drugs can cause the release of large amounts of dopamine. After a time of continued use this release happens in response not only to the drug, but also to things that the brain associates with the use of the drug. Hence, we can see how something that we associate with drug use becomes a trigger.

These are the reasons why the term used after a successful treatment is "recovery" and not that the addict is "cured." From what I have been told, the euphoria produced by these drugs is beyond comprehension. While initially it is this feeling of euphoria that attracts the user to their drug, once addiction has set in, it is the dopamine-glutamate combination that takes over the need to use. Once there, the choice part of the disease is over and the addict is forever addicted. There are many reasons why the addict initially begins to use. A compulsive disorder is just one. As previously mentioned, genetics may also play a part in the role of self-medication.

We have entered into a new age of therapy. Scientists have reached the conclusion that treatment and working a program alone cannot maintain an addict's recovery. High rates of relapse and overdoses resulting in death have led to this conclusion. The scientists feel that that there should be a drug maintenance program (consisting of abstinence plus a drug to do away with the urges felt by the addict) for those that are chronic relapsers. There are several drugs that researchers feel appropriate for this purpose. If you recall, heroin was the wonder drug that was used to free those who suffered from morphine addiction. As one can see this was not so successful. Technically, I'm wrong. If the purpose of heroin was to get people off of morphine—it was highly successful. But, the disease is not the drug that one is addicted to. Addiction is the disease and the drug use is the symptom. Therefore getting someone off of morphine by substituting it with heroin is like curing their allergy by stopping their sneezing by giving them a stuffed nose.

Then came methadone. This was the next wonder drug brought about by Big Pharma to maintain those patients that were addicted to heroin—Dolophine is manufactured by Eli Lilly. In the 1900s, it was initially manufactured as an opiate analgesic (pain reliever) and found to be somewhat successful in the treatment of opiate addiction. It was used often to keep the addict from entering into withdrawal while they were on their way to the United States Narcotic Farm, which opened in 1935 and was an experimental treatment center in Lexington, Kentucky (there were very few treatment centers back in the fifties and sixties). The problem was that the methadone clinics back then were not government run and corruption was rampant. Plus, clients soon found that it was much harder to kick methadone than heroin.

There was then a whole new epidemic that the nation faced: the addiction to methadone. There was a slippery side business as well: addicts who chose to remain heroin addicts quickly realized they could pretend they wanted to come clean by using methadone, frequent the clinic for their portion of methadone and then sell it, thus having money to purchase more heroin. If you can find it, the documentary *Methadonia* illustrates how this happened.

Methadone clinics still exist in certain areas of the country. Keep in mind that your loved one is not in recovery when on methadone: they are addicted to a new drug and an overdose is still possible. Though there are those who legitimately use this as a maintenance medication with some success, as we just learned, it can easily be abused. For the most part, this has not been a successful method of treatment. There is a potential for serious side effects such as changes in learning ability, cognitive changes, and memory loss. According to researchers at the Center for Substance Abuse University of Maryland quoted in *Science Daily*, there is also the possibility of overdose especially if the client combines the methadone with other substances.

The new drugs that we use now are the blockers. These are the Subutex-type drugs such as Suboxone (buprenorphine combined with naloxone) which are a combination of an opiate analgesic and a blocker to prevent the effects of the buprenorphine, hopefully preventing an overdose should the addicted person on this program abuse them.

So, do maintenance drugs benefit the addict, or are they just an easy alternative to fighting to remain sober? Truthfully, that is a question that can only be answered by the person who suffers from the disease. My feeling is that to truly be in recovery the addict must be drug free. I have gained extensive knowledge of the disease but will never understand the emotional feelings that the addict encounters along their journey toward recovery.

What I do know: the relapse rate is very high, approximately 60% on the record. Deaths from overdose are very high (67,367 in 2018), and the potential for abuse and overdose from the maintenance medications is high, too. From what I have experienced, most addicts on maintenance treatment live from day to day as does the addict who works a program without the aid of the maintenance drugs. One of the drawbacks of maintenance programs is that euphoria is missing. For this reason, addicts often seek out other drugs while using this program of replacement drugs so that they can feel the euphoric effect again. This can lead to overdose.

Whether or not an addict should go on a maintenance program is something that your loved one should discuss with their therapist before going to see an addiction doctor. Again, there are doctors who could care less about your loved one, so knowing a little about the doctors in various treatment centers may be helpful in making an informed decision about the best place for your loved one to seek treatment.

If I were pinned to the wall and forced to direct someone, I would say to addicts: *choose total abstinence and work a program.* It is just as easy to relapse in a maintenance program while taking a drug substitute as it is while in a recovery program. A maintenance program is not considered a recovery program and I have seen far too many addicts abusing their maintenance medications by taking too many or selling them. Technically, one cannot relapse if they are not in recovery. So how does someone on a maintenance program relapse? Technically they don't, they exchange one drug for another. For example, they are using Suboxone maintenance once or twice a day and suddenly pick up a bag of heroin and use again. Technically this is not a relapse as they never entered into recovery but let's just say it was "their recovery" while it was working. Then this is a relapse as they have altered their pattern of functioning.

The reason I have suggested being cautiously selective when it comes to choosing a physician (especially should your loved one decide to take the route of the maintenance medication) is that a specialist in this field of medicine can make a big difference. For example, they will do blood tests, and take other steps to ascertain whether the patient is correctly working the maintenance program. Some will do this for the right reasons and some will do this to just stay on the right side of the law.

There are those doctors specializing in the field of addiction that take their profession seriously and do the testing to make sure that your loved one is following the prescribed regimen and if they find that the drug is being abused, will either take steps to get them back on track or discharge them as patients. Then there are those doctors that are just concerned that your loved ones return to the office monthly, performs the prescribed testing so that they remain in compliance with the rules and regulations and have little regard for the patient's outcome. They may not keep accurate records, or as in the case of my daughter, prescribed alprazolam (Xanax) for her anxiety. Like every other professional, some are excellent, some are bad and some fall in the middle. Get advice from the treatment center if possible or the medical association.

So this chapter is about when this epidemic really started. In my opinion, an epidemic starts when it comes to the attention of the populace. If nobody cares about something, chances are it will not be brought to anyone's attention as the press doesn't make money printing stories about things that won't grab the readers' attention. So, an epidemic is not an epidemic if it is not perceived as one. "If something is not perceived, does it exist?", mentioned in the book *Physics* by Charles Ribory and George Ransom Twiss, sheds light on this.

The CDC says that the first wave of the epidemic began with the overdose deaths involving prescription opioids. The second wave began in 1999 with the increase of deaths due to heroin overdose. In my opinion, heroin use was popular back in the 1960s both in the inner city and among the returning Vietnam veterans. Perhaps statics were blurred by improper record keeping or misstatements of cause of death. Let's just suppose Joe Smith returns from Viet Nam totally hooked on heroin. He tires of the lifestyle, so he goes to the VA hospital and tries to enter into a hospital for treatment. He is told they will call him when an opening arises. While he is waiting, he overdoses and dies. He is brought to the medical examiner's office, they go through his wallet and see that he is a veteran and contact the VA hospital for input. They are told that he was an addict and waiting for a bed. The medical examiner notes cause of death "residual psychosis from battle fatigue." Not a lie, but not the truth either.

Opiates were being abused long before the advent of pill mills. As previously stated, I feel the problem was that no one really cared about another person unless they had a personal stake in the problem. Yes, some baby boomers may say, "Oh how terrible alcohol and drugs are." Yet with the new affluence, their children were affected, and some children were even able to pay for their appointments without the knowledge of their parents. When their use was so far advanced that it could no longer be hidden, the tendency was for the parents to deny there was a problem. It was so much easier to believe that this was a stage or rite of passage that children go through. By the time we realized our loved ones could no longer function, we had an epidemic on our hands.

Are we to blame? Not exactly! No one can make someone use but themselves. You are not responsible for their use or their stopping. You may be responsible for contributing to their situation by enabling as this is something that we are all guilty of at one time or another.

I did not write this book to blame anybody. I wrote it to show you that you are not alone and that you are not responsible for what has occurred to your loved one. Guilt and shame are responsible for the negative feelings for everyone involved. You're going to have these feelings and therefore are going need help to overcome them. This is not something that most family members are willing to admit to. Remember this is a family disease and just as the addicted member in the family needs therapy and to work a program to enter into recovery, so too will you.

It is very hard to deal with a family member that is in active addiction. They wreak havoc on most people that they come in contact with and can cause them to make decisions that would not be reached under normal circumstances. You often are driven to feelings of guilt brought on by your thoughts such as *should I ask them to leave?* Remember, sainthood is not bestowed upon those that destroy their lives trying to be the savior. There are no "right answers" that you can look for, either. Should you decide to make your loved one leave your home, you will have some peace but will also be in constant fear of whether or not they are surviving. Should they overdose and don't survive after you have evicted them, you are going to feel guilty. If this happens while you are allowing them to reside in your residence, you are going to wonder if it was your fault for enabling them.

The bottom line is, you must do what you believe is right at the time. Try to not enable your loved one and encourage them to get help. You have the right to live a normal and peaceful existence free from the stress that your addicted love ones will bring to your home. Most importantly, you will need someone to help you deal with your emotional feelings and a support group will help you. You are only permitted shame *if you do not seek help.*

As I was told by a good friend, a tough but gentle man who was a street addict for many years, "If Z doesn't kill herself first, she will eventually tire of the lifestyle and get help for herself." His wish for me was that I would still be around when this occurred. You should never give up the hope that your loved one will attain long-term sobriety. As treatment methods evolve, the results are becoming more positive and you have a brighter future to look towards.

Epilogue: Effective Boundaries and Good News

Yes, I did receive good news today from my daughter. I am sending this as an addition to my editor, who I hope will accept this and not sit there thinking *this guy is a mega pain in the rump*. The last time my daughter came to visit with her boyfriend, the scene was not a pretty one. It ended with me chasing both of them from the house, leaving my wife and me distraught for a couple of days. It was time to set a new boundary and this I did as soon as I was able to contact her. I told her that if she could not visit us sober then we didn't want her to visit at all. It wasn't easy for me to say it. As I explained at that next Family Night meeting: although I don't always express myself emotionally, I do have feelings. When you love your child, even one who is in active addiction, telling them that they can no longer come to visit is a hard, although often necessary, step.

This happened a few weeks ago and the dots somehow connected for her, as the other day she called to ask if I could help her get into treatment. I told her that I would check around and see who would take her insurance (a Florida Medicaid provider). One of the facilities that I give input at volunteered to help me find a good facility that would accept her—that particular facility did not accept her insurance. I called Z to tell her the good news as I knew he would find a better than decent facility; she replied that *she had already found one and was waiting for them to pick her up.*

At this time, she is in the Detox phase of her treatment. I am extremely happy. Am I sure that this will be the treatment that works for her? Truthfully, I am optimistic as I didn't push her into it. Entering into treatment on your own is always a positive. All I can say is I hope that this will work. If it doesn't, I will keep hoping for her success. There are few constants with this disease but one of them is that you never know which treatment is the one that works.

Postscript

This is a final addition to this book. When a loved one suffers from a disease such as addiction, somewhere in the back of your mind is the distant thought that there is a distinct possibility that they may suffer an overdose that they won't recover from. Perhaps having this knowledge makes it a little easier, should this situation arise. But it does not prepare you at all.

My daughter, whom I loved very much, was a chronic relapser. As I may have previously mentioned, this disease is progressive if left unchecked. Often your loved one will do things that you never thought they were capable of doing. The fact is, if they were in recovery, they would probably never do those things. You must keep in mind that their thought process becomes irrational to us, although to someone in active addiction it might appear to be quite rational as it allows them to move toward getting their drugs. This can, and often does, lead to arrests and incarcerations. This was the case with my daughter. She had been in jail for about two months in one county and then was transferred to another. That county arranged for her to be under house arrest. I was not happy about this, but the deal was approved. One night, we picked her up in the jail parking lot where she had been left. She seemed like a new person. The next day, we took her to meet with her probation officer, who set the rules for her, and for us.

Gradually, we noticed a change. Maybe not that gradual, as she was only home for about two and a half weeks. Having developed a greater knowledge of the disease over many years, I began to notice signs of a dry relapse. She became agitated and spoke of using again, once her house arrest time was over. I thought that maybe this would pass or that her parole officer would pick up on it. Neither had time to happen. This morning, at about 8:30am on June 27, 2022, my wife went into her room to ask if she wanted breakfast and found her, slumped over in her bed. She called me and I administered CPR. In a matter of minutes, the paramedics had arrived and pronounced her dead. The removal process took about two hours.

Yes, I had prepared myself for this trauma. Did this preparation help? I don't know. I do know that for the first time in years, I shed tears. Up until today, I felt that only time would tell if she would ever enter into recovery. Over the years, my hope for this seemed to wane, although I never *stopped* hoping. My wife and I will grieve, but over time the grieving process will hopefully lessen our pain. The brain is a very special organ. It has ways to help us to recover from these situations—my final words to you.

About the Author

Lawrence Fish, RPh, is a retired pharmacist who re-thought his entire life when his daughter "Z" fell ill with addiction. She started as a casual user, so her descent was not perceivable initially—and a call from the police catapulted him, his wife, and Z onto a whole new trajectory no one was prepared for. Only after she completed her first treatment, did Fish realize that he—like most other family members of a sufferer—knew so little about this insidious disease.

Parental guilt took its toll, initially. Even Fish's professional training taught him virtually nothing about the world of addiction, how his daughter was suffering, and what she would encounter in her future. After Z's first relapse, he continued to attend the treatment center's Family Night meetings and developed a passion for in-depth learning about this disease.

This real-life education led him to open the Fifty-Fifty House, a sober living facility in Pompano Beach, Florida, where weekly meetings connected to the greater Narcotics Anonymous community became a new source of knowledge. With insight gained from attending two to three meetings per week for the past fifteen-plus years, Fish continues to actively participate in meetings and is dedicated to helping other parents, family members, and caregivers who find themselves in a position of supporting an adult child or family member with addiction.

Email him at pharfish@aol.com.

Publisher's Note

Thank you for the opportunity to serve you. If you would like to help share this message, here are some popular ways:

- **Reviews:** Write an online book review

- **Giving:** Gift this book to friends, family, and colleagues

- **Reading Groups:** Read this book with your support group and invite Lawrence Fish, RPh, to attend the meeting in person or via video conference. Email pharfish@aol.com.

- **Speaking:** Invite Lawrence Fish, RPh, to speak with your organization. Email pharfish@aol.com.

- **Bulk Orders:** Email sales@citrinepublishing.com

- **Contact Information:** Call +1-828-585-7030 or email: info@citrinepublishing.com

We appreciate your book reviews, letters, and shares.

www.ingramcontent.com/pod-product-compliance
Lightning Source LLC
Chambersburg PA
CBHW030149100526
44592CB00009B/187